Philosophy of Education Research Library

Series Editors
  V. A. Howard and Israel Scheffler
  Harvard Graduate School of Education

Recent decades have witnessed the decline of distinctively philosophical thinking about education. Practitioners and the public alike have increasingly turned rather to psychology, the social sciences and to technology in search of basic knowledge and direction. However, philosophical problems continue to surface at the center of educational concerns, confronting educators and citizens as well with inescapable questions of value, meaning, purpose, and justification.

PERL will publish works addressed to teachers, school administrators and researchers in every branch of education, as well as to philosophers and the reflective public. The series will illuminate the philosophical and historical bases of educational practice, and assess new educational trends as they emerge.

Already published

Language, Ability and Educational Achievement

Language, Ability and Educational Achievement

Christopher Winch

Routledge
New York   London

Published in 1990 by

Routledge
An imprint of Routledge, Chapman and Hall, Inc.
29 West 35 Street
New York, NY 10001

Published in Great Britain by

Routledge
11 New Fetter Lane
London EC4P 4EE

Library of Congress Cataloging-in-Publication Data
Winch, Christopher.
    Language ability and educational achievement / by Christopher
Winch.
        p.   cm.—(Philosophy of education research library)
    Includes bibliographical references.
    ISBN 0-415-90226-6
    1. Academic achievement.   2. Language and education.   3. Children-
-Intelligence levels.   4. Verbal ability in children.   5. Education-
-Social aspects.   I. Title.   II. Series.
LB1062.6.W56   1990
370.15—dc20
                                                                89-31840

Contents

Acknowledgments

I would like to thank the editors of the "Journal of Philosophy of Education", the "Journal of Applied Philosophy" and the "Oxford Review of Education" for permission to use material previously published in those journals, notably the "Journal of Philosophy of Education" 1983 V. 17, No. 2 and 1988 V. 22, No. 1; the "Journal of Applied Philosophy" 1985, V. 2, No. 1 and 1988 V. 5, No. 2 and the "Oxford Review of Education" 1985, V. 11, No. 2.

Introduction

The subject of this book is educational achievement. Ever since records have been kept, it has been noticed that some children respond better to teaching than others. Some children learn more than others and learn more quickly. Some children have a greater interest in their studies and are more keen to learn than others.

The advent of mass education in the nineteenth century brought another, related phenomenon into focus. There appears to be a significant relationship between social class and educational achievement. In particular, there appears to be a persistent connection between belonging to low-prestige social groups and relatively low educational achievement. Many educators have thought that the phenomenon of group differences and the phenomenon of individual differences in achievement are closely connected, and theories have been advanced to explain both of these phenomena in a satisfactory way.

Why should philosophy interest itself in such theories? One answer to this question goes as follows. Ways of explaining educational success are concerned with matters of fact, namely, why some children achieve more than others while they are at school. To explain these matters of fact, ideas that have a familiar life in everyday usage are introduced in a technical way into psychology, sociology, and linguistics in order to contribute to theories that explain different educational achievement. Some expressions have a technical origin, pass into everyday usage, and are then reappropriated by specialists.

We are all familiar with such terms as "able," "competent," "intelligent," "equal," "deprived," and "interest" in their day-to-day usage. When we are confronted with the corresponding abstract nouns: "ability," "competence," "intelligence," "equality," and "deprivation," we may think that we are on familiar ground, for we can understand "John has great ability" to mean "John is very able at such and such an activity." If, however, a psychologist were to introduce a technical notion of ability as a human quality and were to claim that we could measure it in an individual, compare its occurrence in different people, or trace its development through a person's lifetime, then we should be aware of two questions. First, is the new notion of ability a straightforward extension of our everyday concept? That is, in the psychologist's usage, does "ability" in "John has great ability" still have a clear and intelligible relation to "ability" in our everyday use of that word? Second, is this new use of "ability" of any use to us, does it even have a clear application that will help us to find out more about people and what they can and cannot do?

Neither of these two questions is a scientific one. They cannot be settled by conducting surveys or experiments, but by attention to our ways of talking and thinking, and this is a type of investigation in which philosophy has a real interest. Equally to the point, if we are not sure whether or not the psychologist's new use of "ability" is intelligible or useful, how can we know whether or not the theories he or she constructs about educational achievement have any value in explaining it? We can see, therefore, that philosophy may have something to say to the world of contemporary educational concerns in looking critically and in detail at the way we pursue those concerns. Such an enterprise is no less important than that of the empirical investigator—indeed, if his or her work is to succeed, it is necessary that the questions asked and the theories formulated have a reasonably clear sense if they are to be of any use to us.

Technical concepts that have been introduced into the world of educational debate and research about educational achievement are, then, the main concern of this book. Chapter 1 provides a brief historical introduction to the topic under discussion. Chapter 2 deals with intelligence, rationality, and language, and Chapter 3 with culture and interest. Chapters 4 through 6 examine theories of intelligence that have been particularly influential in the field of education. Chapters 7 through 11 look at another influential group of theories about educational achievement, one centered on notions of language deficit and deprivation. Chapter 12 takes a closer look at the concept of equality, and Chapter 13 draws some conclusions from the discussion and provides a broad summary of the issues.

CHAPTER 1

Historical introduction

There is nothing new about the idea that people vary in the kind and degree of ability they possess and that these variations in ability determine the kind of education (if any) that they receive as well as their general situation in life. The ancient Greek philosopher Plato (427–347 B.C.) in the *Republic* (Plato 1950) describes an ideal city-state in which the citizens are assigned an education and position in life that suits their characters and abilities. Such procedures, Plato maintains, are essential to the safety and well-being of the city-state. Apart from their intrinsic interest, Plato's descriptions of the *Republic* and its different types of citizen have a relevance to contemporary discussions, one that I hope to bring out in the course of this book.

Plato distinguishes between three types of people in the ideal city-state: the guardians or rulers, the auxiliaries or defenders against external enemies, and the productive class of artisans and agriculturalists. Corresponding to these three classes of people are three qualities of the human soul, each associated with a different kind of person. The first, figuratively associated with the metal gold, is the rational element; it is associated with the guardians. The spirited or passionate element (associated with silver) is connected with the martial and physically robust side of human nature and hence with the soldier–citizens; iron and copper are associated with human appetite, with need and desire, and with the artisan and farming class of people. In a division between the rational and the appetitive principles, the spirited principle always aligns itself with the rational principle.

Note that Socrates, who is speaking for Plato, puts forward this story as an agreeable fiction in order to convince the citizens of the city-state that the ordering of society is just. It is clear, however, that although a fiction, the account is also a reasonable approximation of Plato's view of the constitution of the human soul. There are three important points about Plato's discussion worth bearing in mind. The first is that the qualities of mind, or at least their distribution, are inherited, but mental characteristics are not always passed on intact from one generation to another:

> Therefore inasmuch as you are all related to one another, although all your children will generally resemble their parents, yet sometimes a golden parent

will produce a silver child, and a silver parent a golden child, and so on, each producing any. (Plato 1950, 114)

If each can produce any, the rulers and their assistants will have to select children very carefully on their observed merits, in order to ensure that the right sort of person does the right sort of job. Second, Plato does not believe that merely because one has it in one to become a ruler or a soldier, it will necessarily follow that one will become one without a most careful and rigorous education. In other words, what one has it in one to be needs to be realized by an appropriate kind of education.

Third, the kind of education that Plato considers appropriate for a guardian, the possessor of the most noble type of soul, is an abstract and contemplative one, exemplified by the study of philosophy. The cultivation of theoretical reason as the highest good in education can be traced at least back to Plato; its consequences are very much with us to this day and are in fact at the center of current educational debates (e.g., Donaldson 1978, O'Hear 1985, Abbs 1987). The claims of theoretical reason and practical reason, sometimes competing, sometimes harmonious, will constitute one of the major themes of this book.

Plato's ideas have tended to support a generally hereditarian and hierarchical view of intellectual ability (e.g., Burt 1955, 182–204); Jean-Jacques Rousseau (1712–78), on the other hand, forcibly expressed the view that it is the social environment rather than inherited characteristics that account for the unequal distribution of social position and reward:

It is in fact easy to see that many of the differences which distinguish men are merely the effect of habit and the different methods of life men adopt in society. Thus a robust or delicate constitution, and the strength or weakness attaching to it, are more frequently the effects of a hardy or effeminate method of education than of the original endowment of the body. It is the same with powers of the mind; for education not only makes a difference between such as are cultured and such as are not, but even increases the differences which exist among the former, in proportion to their respective degrees of culture: as the distance between a giant and a dwarf on the same road increases with every step they take. If we compare the prodigious diversity, which obtains in the education and manner of life of the various orders of men in the state of society, with the uniformity and simplicity of animal and savage life, in which every one lives in exactly the same manner and does exactly the same things, it is easy to conceive how much less the difference between man and man must be in the state of nature than in a state of society, and how greatly the natural inequality of mankind must be increased by the inequality of social institutions. (Rousseau 1754, available in Cole, ed., 1968, pp. 188–189)

Both Platonic and Rousseauist standpoints are central to debates about ability and educational achievement. They form the basis of the two principal opposing points of view in the so-called "nature–nurture dispute"—that is, the dispute as to whether or not human abilities are predominantly inherited or acquired. With the advent of mass education in the nineteenth century, the Rousseauist view (shared by other eighteenth-century Enlightenment thinkers) largely prevailed. Poor educational achievement, it was held, could be ascribed to poor teaching and moral as opposed to intellectual deficiencies among parents and children (cf. Gordon 1981). An alternative view was beginning to emerge under the influence of the Social Darwinist thinker Herbert Spencer. This alternative was essentially a revival of the Platonic idea of hereditary innate intelligence and received vigorous expression in the work of Francis Galton. Galton states:

> I have no patience with the hypothesis occasionally expressed and often implied, especially in tales written to teach children to be good, that babies are born pretty much alike, and that the sole agencies in creating differences between boy and boy, and man and man, are steady application and moral effort. It is in the most unqualified manner that I object to pretensions of natural equality. (Galton 1892, 25)

In the years after the First World War, the science of psychometry and, specifically, that of the measurement of intelligence, which embodied hereditarian ideas about natural ability, came to dominate educational thinking, overshadowing the earlier Victorian view of natural equality—which was itself influenced by the thinkers of the Enlightenment. It is worth pointing out that another feature of the Platonic heritage, the idea that there are different types of mind, also revived and is notable in the Norwood Report (1943), which recommended different types of schools for different types of mind. It is no exaggeration to say that the eleven-plus selection system and the division between grammar, technical, and secondary modern schools in the United Kingdom was heavily influenced by psychometric ideas.

Psychometry has gone into decline as a major means for assessing educational potential and type of education. Its value for predicting educational success is now doubted by many. Very damagingly, one of its main exponents, Sir Cyril Burt, is suspected to have presented fraudulent evidence for certain aspects of the theory (cf. Hearnshaw 1979). More generally, as Gordon (1981) has noted, the deterministic and static view of human potential displayed by psychometric accounts of ability has gone against the social optimism and the demand for a skilled and educated workforce that have predominated since the Second World War.

From the mid-1950s until the present, a new cluster of "verbal-deficit" theories has emerged to explain class-related differences in educational achievement. These theories, notably associated with the work of Basil Bernstein, postulate differences in the social and cultural environment as a major determinant of educational achievement. A poor environment breeds an inferior form of language and thinking, which in turn accounts for poor educational achievement. Although apparently opposed to the hereditarian views of the psychometrists, verbal-deficit theories have quite a lot in common with theories of intelligence. This book will devote some space to disentangling the often close connections that exist between the two groups of theories.

Both intelligence and verbal-deficit theories have a determinist bias to them—that is, they propose factors beyond the control of the individual as crucial to his or her success. Both verbal-deficit and intelligence views have, in some versions, lent themselves to the idea that there are different kinds of mind.

Verbal-deficit theories have themselves aroused much controversy and have come under attack. There is now no single orthodoxy of views about the causes of differing educational achievement among different social groups, but there are a number of points of view and different lines of research. Among these lines of research the most promising seems to be inquiry into the connection between literacy and cultural background (cf.Donaldson 1978, Tizard and Hughes 1984, Wells 1987). It will be suggested in Chapter 12 that a point of view that takes into account the importance of literacy and culturally based interest is probably the most illuminating way of seeing the phenomenon of different educational achievement.

It is beyond the scope of this book and, indeed, beyond the scope of philosophy to provide an answer to the problems of educational achievement. What such a book may be able to do is to uncover some of the issues surrounding the various theories and to examine whether or not those theories are coherently formulated. This is not a marginal exercise. If a theory is not coherently formulated, then there is little point in putting it to an empirical test. It will be seen, however, that there are many conceptual problems both with the formulation of the theories under discussion and with the ways in which they are tested, and that these theories, dealing as they do with concepts of philosophical interest such as intelligence, language, and so on, allow philosophy ample opportunity for illuminating comment on their value.

CHAPTER 2

Intelligence, language, and learning

Intelligence

Before we can ask the question "What is intelligence?" it might be better first to pose the question, "Can there be anything that goes under the name 'Intelligence'?" In other words, can we understand "Intelligence" as an abstract noun referring to some (as yet unspecified) quality of the mind? Burt has with some justification pointed to the technical pedigree of the term from the writings of Plato and Aristotle to Cicero (Burt 1955, 183–84), but, as is often the case, the term and in particular its grammatical associates have passed into common usage and are used more or less synonymously in certain contexts with "clever," "smart," "able," "bright," "good," and so on.

We have no difficulty with such expressions as "He is an intelligent footballer" or "She handled that parent in an intelligent manner," which suggest a disposition of the footballer or the headteacher to behave in certain ways highly appropriate to the activities in which they are engaging. Psychologists, however, often mean by "intelligence" a general property of the mind, and we are justified in asking whether or not the term does in fact refer to an important unitary property of minds, for this is what is often claimed, particularly by theorists of intelligence.

One cannot infer a single mental property of intelligence just by reflecting on ordinary usage. Where "intelligence" is used, it can be taken usually as a paraphrase for "intelligent F" (where "F" is a term standing for some kind of human activity). We can, however, look for some general traits of intelligent behavior. Thus, for example, attention is drawn to a flexibility and adaptability of response (Bennett 1964) or to the ability to see connections (White 1974). These traits can be seen as complementary, and others, also expressive of behavior appropriate to a particular activity, can be added. "Good," "able," "clever," and so on are also used to describe activity or behavior that is highly apt in a particular context or particularly well-executed.

One can draw attention to sympathy and interpretative vision in a musician, to an eye for detail and a capacity to take pains in an administrator, quick-wittedness in a lawyer, psychological insight in a detective, an eye for terrain in a military commander, and so on. In drawing attention to these traits, I do not mean to imply that they are interior or unobservable discrete mental acts that somehow constitute the behavior as intelligent. Nor do I mean to imply that these traits are necessarily exclusive to the activities to which I have just ascribed them. However, our *understanding* of what these traits are will vary from activity to activity. Thus, a capacity to take pains may be a trait of an able musician as well as of an administrator. We would tend to ascribe it to a musician who, for example, practiced diligently, or who took great care in selecting an instrument, whereas the administrator who took pains might be said to do so because he was methodical and cautious in the *actual execution* of his work.

These traits can be grouped together in certain cases and separated in others to form families of complementary and contrasting characteristics of behavior appropriate to a particular activity. For example, the intuitive grasp and boldness of initiative of a good footballer is less obviously an appropriate set of traits for an activity that requires careful observation and deliberation before action is taken—by a snooker player, for example. This is not to say that boldness and intuitive grasp are not necessarily characteristics of good snooker players, but that they are less prominently so and have a different manifestation in the snooker hall in comparison with the football pitch.

The terms "intelligent" or "clever" are also used in a fairly general way to talk about the variety of response in animals. For example, if we say that a fly is less intelligent or less clever than a dog, we mean roughly that the fly has a more rigid pattern of behavior and a less flexible set of responses than a dog, rather than that the dog does certain things better than the fly. Nor do we imply that the fly has some fixed quantity of "intelligence" than a dog, but to a lesser degree.

Another point about the use of expressions that indicate and evaluate behavior according to how well it fits an activity is its *normative* character—that is, they are used to indicate and evaluate behavior as *more* or *less* appropriate to an activity. "Intelligent" also has a *constitutive* use as in "Some animals are intelligent but no machines are," where "intelligent" is used to indicate the presence of a property of animals in contrast to its absence in machines, without implying anything as to degree or quality (a point made by White 1974).

It might, however, be said that perhaps ordinary usage is a poor guide and that "intelligence" should properly refer to a unitary property of the mind (Spearman 1904) or a hierarchical structure of abilities (Burt 1949) whose nature can be uncovered by scientific investigation. This is a question that I will attempt to answer in Chapter 6. In the meantime, we need to turn to language and communication before discussing rationality. A discussion of language and rationality is necessary for the proper understanding of both verbal-deficit theories and theories of intelligence.

Language

It is well known that many animal species have some means of communicating with each other—that is, some specialized way of conveying information from one member of the species to another or of expressing a feeling or an emotion. For example, there are warning signals and mating dances among mammals. Even among some kinds of insects there are highly developed systems of communication, for instance the "dancing" behavior of bees to convey information as to the whereabouts of food.

It is natural to contrast such behavior with the use of language. Just how this contrast is made is a difficult problem, and perhaps it is a mistake to try to demarcate the use of language from other forms of communication too sharply, for fear of ending up with an overly rigid conception of what language must be. Perhaps it would be better to talk of a continuum of communicative behavior from the most limited forms of animal communication to the languages that humans speak. It is true that some species have evolved complex ways of conveying information, some of it resembling in certain respects the complexity of human linguistic behavior. Bees again are a good example of this phenomenon (cf. Bennett 1964), as is the colony of chimpanzees who took over the sign language Ameslan for their own use (cf. Midgley 1980).

Communicative behavior comes to resemble human languages to the extent that it enables a flexibility and novelty of response in a wide variety of situations. Thus the communication of bees, although possessing a certain kind of complexity (a lot of different messages can be conveyed by subtly different forms of "dance"), is also very rigidly circumscribed. Communication relates to one subject, food, and only concerns its distance, direction, and concentration. There is no give and take of communicative exchange, no way of conveying information about different sorts of situations potentially of interest to the bees (for example, danger), no way of backing up a "dance" with evidence, no way of expressing disagreement or detecting untruth, and so on. Communication becomes more language-like to the extent that it becomes more adaptable to the variety of a species' needs, can help to make sense of a new situation, can adapt to changes in the environment and the needs of the species itself, and to the point where it allows learning to take place so as to make the communication itself of more value to the species. For example, can the creatures learn to distrust a consistently untruthful communicator? Can they ask for reasons and evidence for statements? Can they doubt or deny what is said and investigate the truth of what is communicated to them? These sorts of features in a system of communication, possibly with an increase in the number and complexity of signs used, would tend to make us inclined to say that the communication was becoming more language-like. They would not however commit us to saying "Language must be like this . . . ," followed by a list of necessary conditions for a system of communication to constitute a language.

Rationality

Since the time of Aristotle, it has been a commonplace to describe humans as rational animals. "Rationality," like "intelligence," is a semi-technical term that has found its way into common usage; also like "intelligence," it has a certain amount of ambiguity as to its meaning. Being rational is sometimes equated with the ability to reason, and the ability to reason is, in turn, connected with the use of language.

Bennett (1964) in particular tried to show how "rationality" and "reason" were bound up with the linguistic faculty of being able to talk about matters not in the immediate spatiotemporal context and hence with the use of temporal expressions and words such as "all" and "some." Midgley (1980), on the other hand, has emphasized the use of "rational" to refer to preferences bound up with the nature of the human species. These include not only physical needs but also specifically human traits such as a preference for company, ceremony, entertainment, agreeable surroundings, and so on. It would also be a feature of rationality to keep a balance and a set of relative values among preferences so that, for example, one preference does not crowd out others to the detriment of the individual:

> Practical reasoning would be impossible were not some preferences more rational than others. Rationality includes having the right priorities. And deep, lasting preferences linked to character traits are formally quite a different proposition from sharp isolated impulses. (Midgley 1980, 259)

"Rational" in connection with reasoning is clearly bound up with the ability to use language. It is evident that our ability to reason and our associated ability to speak are distinctive features of humanity. They are also what make intelligent human behavior different from the intelligent behavior of animals. We can say, therefore, that the human intellect is primarily exercised through rational thought and behavior and that language is therefore brought into the picture in a fundamental way.

However, the concept of rationality does have various aspects that are well worth distinguishing before we come to understand the claims of I.Q. and verbal-deficit theories. It has already been noted that certain features of language allow humans to engage in certain sorts of thinking; in particular, the availability of expressions such as "if . . . then . . . ," "not . . . ," ". . . and . . . ," and "either . . . or . . . ," permit a variety of inferences, whereas expressions such as "all . . . ," and "some . . ." allow a further range of arguments to be used. It is an important and interesting fact about human languages that they all appear to share roughly the same structural characteristics, a fact that has been remarked for some time by linguists. Lyons states:

> It is still fairly common to hear laymen talking about "primitive" languages, and repeating the myth that there are some peoples whose language consists of a couple of hundred words supplemented by gestures. The truth is that every language so far studied, no matter how "backward" or "uncivilized" the people speaking it, has proved on investigation to be a complex and highly developed system of communication. Moreover, there is absolutely no correlation between the different stages of cultural development through which these societies have "evolved" and the "type" of language spoken in these stages of cultural development. (Lyons 1968, 44)

Although it is theoretically possible for there to be a variety of structurally different forms of language, each expressing a capacity for more or less rich forms of thinking about the world, it seems that linguists, with the evidence of field research among the different peoples of the world, have not found any such "simple" language in existence.

On the other hand, if verbal-deficit theorists are to be believed, then there may well exist such structural variation *within* our own language and languages like it. We will try to make sense of this apparent difference of opinion in Chapters 7 through 11. Our ability to use language to express thoughts of a certain variety and complexity can be called *constitutive rationality*. Constitutive rationality of a certain degree is something that a person either possesses, or does not possess.

By contrast, that feature of rationality drawn attention to by Midgley, which refers to our practical abilities in organizing interest and preference and realizing such things in the physical and social world around us, is something that we can be more or less good at in different ways. Consider, for example, the ability to carry through a commercial project and all the expertise that it might require: knowledge of finance, negotiating skills, the ability to make rapid judgments on important matters, and so on. It is clear that some people are better than others at realizing practical projects of this nature. On the other hand, one's ability as a practical reasoner may vary from one context to another. For example, a good businessman may not be very good at organizing his personal preferences and personal life. Ingenuity and skill at the invention of useful and potentially profitable gadgets may not be coupled with any acumen in persuading people with money to invest in their potential value. More starkly, an ability to advise people on how to assess and sort out their own personal lives may not be matched by the ability to do the same with one's own life.

Thus, not only is practical rationality a matter of "more or less," but it is patterned across different contexts in different ways for different people. This is because, for each of the activities that humans engage in, there are different sorts of means–ends relationships, different sorts of skills and attitudes involved, different sorts of relationships with other people, and different institutional and customary backgrounds to the activities. People bring to their participation in, say, football, farming, and domestic life not only their knowledge of and aptitude for the activity but also a personal and cultural background of interest and sympathy (of which more in Chapter 3) that all come together to make someone a more or less adept practitioner of an activity. This contextually patterned aspect of practical reasoning can be called *contextual rationality*.

The practical exercise of rationality involved in making decisions and carrying them out is complemented by a more reflective ability, and it is sometimes useful to distinguish this ability from our decision-making ability. This more reflective ability is our capacity to give and to assess reasons for the truth of a statement, to build up or criticize an argument, and generally to make judgments as to truth, the advisability of a course of action, and so on.

Of course, such a distinction between judging and making decisions is, to a certain extent, artificial, as in real life the two abilities turn out much of the time to be nothing more than two aspects of the same ability. However, the practical and *argumentative* aspects of rationality do not always run in parallel tracks, and argumentative rationality enjoys a certain autonomy from the practical aspect of rationality and vice versa. Inferences from premises to conclusions are good or bad, valid or invalid, independent of whether or not the conclusion fits in with what we would like to believe or would wish to do. This is a point whose importance will emerge in Chapter 10.

The logic of inference can be studied in a formal and systematic fashion, without reference to reasoning in a practical context. When principles of reasoning are systematized and perhaps put in a symbolic form, then some aspects of the everyday activities of inductive and deductive reasoning can be studied as a branch of mathematics. It should be noted, however, that these formal systems capture only part of the complexity and subtlety of everyday inference, and that they should be used with great care to describe the operation of inference in natural languages (cf. Blackburn 1984, 293–301). *Argumentative* rationality, like the *deliberative* rationality of decision making, can be something that different people are more or less good at and good at in different ways. For example, an adept in the cut and thrust of informal argument is not necessarily going to be even *slightly* competent in symbolic logic, and the same point applies vice versa.

What is the connection between this discussion of rationality and our concern with education? To start with, education might be said to have as a major aim the development of rationality. But the question at once arises: which aspect of rationality? For if the linguists are right and the fundamental structure of all languages have the same degree of complexity, and we further suppose that normally healthy people are competent in the use of their native language, then education is little concerned with the development of constitutive rationality, unless we are talking about the field of special education. If some forms of verbal-deficit theory are correct, however, education may be very much concerned with the development of constitutive rationality.

Education, therefore, might be seen as having as one of its goals the development of the constitutive rationality of some children; it will certainly play an important part, however, in the development of different contextual rationalities through the acquisition of knowledge and skill in different subject areas. The relative importance of the development of the theoretical and practical aspects of rationality will also be a matter for debate among educationists and policymakers, as indeed it has already been for centuries. Regarding the focus of this book, we can be more specific. Verbal-deficit theories make claims about the capacities of a speaker's language for expressing rationality. But, as we shall see in Chapters 7 through 10, these claims are highly ambiguous and, until they have been cleared up, cannot lead to a satisfactory account of why some groups achieve more, educationally, than others.

We saw earlier how "intelligence" relates to a family of descriptions of what being competent, good, or expert at an activity is like. Most human activities, either implicitly or explicitly, involve language and, therefore, the exercise of constitutive rationality. The use of language is deeply involved in most manifestations of human intellectual endeavor. Even when the activity is not overtly linguistic, as with music, painting, or rock climbing, language is not far in the background. A background of shared language and social experience is part of what makes a person a good musician, painter, or climber, for we relate our description of someone as good at something not merely to their physical performance of a task, but also to their playing a social role in the pattern of human life that goes together with the activity in question, which might involve, for example, discussion, learning, practice, rivalry, mutual help, and a variety of other language-based activities. Either implicitly or explicitly, therefore, rationality and the use of language lie close to the major questions of intellectual achievement and particularly to educational achievement, where language is very often central to the activities that are being learned.

Education can be seen as relevant to the development of constitutive rationality only if some of the strong claims of verbal-deficit theory are correct. The development of theoretical, practical, and contextual rationality can be seen as the proper province of the educator. One thing that should be borne in mind is that the theoretical and practical aspects of rationality, although distinguishable, are closely linked and should be seen most helpfully as two aspects of the same thing. There is no particular virtue in seeing the theoretical aspect of rationality as "higher" than the practical aspect unless there is a cultural bias in society making it so. "Theoretical" and "practical" do not relate to radically different forms of education. Indeed, the idea that they do is one that has arguably bedeviled our education system in the past and has partly contributed to the theories of educational achievement that will be discussed in this book.

CHAPTER 3

Class, culture, and interest

People live socially in communities with various customs, routines, institutions, and rituals; these give rise to a commonality of background, values, and outlook that confers a sense of identity on the members of that community. This social environment can be called a *culture* and is an essential medium of human expression and development, as Midgley (1980) points out.

Modern societies are complex and have a corresponding complexity in their cultures (sociologists speak of subcultures). One helpful way of looking at this complexity is to associate it with the division of labor that a modern society requires. A modern economy requires a vast range of different tasks to be performed and a labor force that is highly specialized. Sociologists group the performers of these various tasks into what is, broadly speaking, a hierarchy of social esteem. These groupings, although inexact, are helpful in giving us a broad view of the differences in education, interests, values, skills, and outlook of members of the different groups. These groupings range from higher administrative, managerial, and professional jobs through clerical and lower-grade administrative functions, through skilled, semiskilled, and unskilled forms of manual work.

These groupings are imperfect; for example, as Rosen (1974) points out, the description of an occupation as skilled very often relates to the success of a group of workers in getting described as "skilled" rather to an objective assessment of the degree of skill involved. Nonetheless, they give us a broad picture of the division of labor in a modern society.

Associated with the division of labor is a tendency for a group to share a common set of values and opinions about the world; these go together with shared material interests, patterns of work, forms of recreation, and family rituals, and—last but not least—a shared experience of educational institutions. So, for example, administrative-grade civil servants, top management, and senior politicians will share family connections through intermarriage, similar conditions of work, and schooling, and will probably share a similar range of leisure and recreational interests.

Factory-workers and their families, on the other hand, might live on housing estates in similar parts of a city, will tend to have left school at the age of fifteen or sixteen (in the United Kingdom), and will have similar experiences of work and responsibility. They may also be members of a trade union. Their leisure and recreational interests will tend to differ from those of the first group and will tend to involve literacy to a far lesser degree.

Two important features of such societies are worth remarking for the moment. The first is that the groups are, to a certain extent, self-perpetuating, that is, children will tend in the main to follow the educational pattern, interests, and occupations of their parents. This phenomenon is a more general case of the phenomenon of different educational achievement noted in the Introduction. It is most important to note that these are *tendencies*, and there remains a considerable degree of generational mobility between social classes, more so in some countries than in others.

The second important feature to note is the extent to which literacy, that is, the practice of using the printed or written rather than the spoken word, plays an important part in the work and more general life experience of some groups of people, and a much less important part in the lives of other groups of people. This tends to introduce a divide between manual and clerical workers, marking off what is sometimes called the "working class" from other groups. One must be careful in making this point. In a modern society, most people are to some extent literate. The experience of literacy varies greatly with occupations. Manual occupations do not involve an *active* use of the literate medium—that is, through writing, typing, and so on—or, at least, do so only to a small extent. Neither should one ignore the distinction between those who merely *process* literary materials for others (e.g., secretaries, typists, and clerical workers) and those whose literary role is to some extent creative: people who prepare briefings, carry out research, prepare minutes, write reports, and so on.

Now that we have briefly looked at social stratification and the cultural differences that can easily be associated with it, it is worth looking at different views as to what underlies stratification and the cultural differences associated with it. Three views will be introduced and described. They are not mutually contradictory, but there is certainly a tension that runs between them that makes them uneasy bedfellows.

The first conception is what could be called the Platonic view of social stratification and cultural differences. This view, although it can be traced back to Plato, is certainly not his alone and is to be found also in the works of Aristotle and in the work of such writers as Burt. The Platonic ideal of society is one that groups people according to their natural ability. The most intelligent members of society are at the peak of the social pyramid and are also the people who have access to philosophical ideas and who carefully control art and recreational activities, which, Plato held, were potentially dangerous to the social order if not carefully watched. Members of lower sections of society lead lives more concerned with the pursuit of need and desire than with the search for knowledge.

A vivid picture of what life for the lower working class in Britain might be like is offered in Bernstein (1973a)—although it should be said that Bernstein's work does not have the hereditarian overtones of the views of I.Q. theorists and of Plato. In the Bernsteinian picture, working-class life is limited to the immediate concerns of home and work, and reference to other matters is difficult if not impossible to achieve. The impoverished language of working-class people contributes to this state of affairs and makes it difficult for their children to benefit from schooling. There is little sense of temporal order; the future is not brought clearly into focus through forward planning or the setting of goals for the future. Life revolves around the temporal present and local surroundings. Personal relationships are largely confined to within-group expressions of solidarity and between-group expressions of distance or even—between working- and middle-class—incomprehension (e.g., Bernstein 1958, 47).

The educated middle class, on the other hand, enjoys a high sense of individuality that is carefully cultivated in the kind of language that they use; it has a sense of reality that goes well beyond the immediate temporal context and allows projects to be carried out that involve forethought and planning for the future. Their language is a much richer and more subtle medium of expression than working-class language.

The Platonic conception of social differences and associated cultural differences rests on the assumption of a different pattern of intellect within the different social classes. Such a view makes the particular social stratification that does occur almost inevitable, as different patterns of intellect are suited for particular kinds of work and culture. The most that can be allowed in this model, if one is not a believer in the hereditary transmission of mental ability, is for a massive cultural transformation of the working class through large-scale programs for educational and linguistic intervention (see Chapter 9).

The second model of social stratification is one that could be called Rousseauist, although it is also closely associated with Marx and his followers. The Rousseauist view is that the small natural differences in intellectual and physical ability that occur in nature become reinforced in society, originally through self-esteem and the desire for the approval of other people, into institutions where inequalities of wealth and opportunity are preserved with the help of the state. The Marxist account differs from the Rousseauist in that it makes the development of class societies based on the division of labor something that is a product of human efforts to master the physical environment. The Rousseauist-Marxist account of social class ascribes its origins and maintenance rather more to *institutions* than to differences in intellectual ability. This set of views does not postulate significant intellectual differences between the two classes as a basis for social differences. The social order is maintained through a judicious mixture of coercion: police, courts, prisons, and army, and the use of ideas and persuasion to convince people that the existing social order is a just one.

Whatever the merits of this picture, its vision of the culture of the lower orders of society, particularly of the industrial working class, differs from that of the Platonic view. As there are no substantial differences in intellectual ability of either degree or kind (social and economic inequality being maintained through institutions such as the police and schools), there is a very different view, particularly in the works of Marx, of the character of working-class life and institutions. The social world is seen as an area of conflict and contestation between the class that owns the means of production (in the present system, the bourgeoisie) and the one that sells its labor power (the working class). In particular, the working class is a body that is capable of forming its own institutions such as trade unions and political parties as political alternatives to the existing order, for the governing of society. Some Marxist writers, notably Gramsci (cf. Gramsci 1975), stress the intellectual character of nearly all human activity and dwell on the need for the working class to develop intellectual leaders from within its own ranks. Paradoxically, it is the very thing that working class and bourgeoisie have in common—namely, the same kind of rationality—that makes their struggle so intense. For according to the Marxist view both see themselves as the rightful rulers of society and both have the intellectual means to act as such. There could be no class struggle if one class were not capable of developing its own institutions and vision of a social order. There would instead be sullenness, spasmodic disobedience, and rioting as tokens of dissatisfaction with a social order that could not be changed in any fundamental way.

Class conflict in the Marxist sense does, then, require cooperation between the classes in production in order to establish a divergence of interest over payment, manning, and work practices over which conflict can arise. In other words, capitalism must have settled into a certain stability before class conflict can take place. This is not to deny that the conflict between the classes may not sometimes be of an irrational and destructive nature, particularly in the early period of capitalism or when a working class is in the process of formation, but this fact does not so much imply a difference in constitutive rationality between the two classes as an inability on one or both sides to properly understand the contextual rationalities of living and working in a system of industrial production.

I do not, at this stage, wish to comment on the relative merits of the Platonic and the Rousseauist-Marxist accounts of social inequality. Instead, I would like to introduce a new horse into the race that may turn out to be a rival or a friend to one of the two views that I have already sketched.

Human beings do not merely ensure their physical survival through their labor, but they produce their conditions of living; these include not only the tools, buildings, and so on that are physically necessary for survival but also customs, institutions, and patterns of activity that provide the social medium of human existence. The human need for company, self-expression, and acceptance by other members of the species are part of human "instinctive" nature just as is the need of other social animals to live together. Language and the possession of what we call "rationality" make a very different kind of social life possible for humans, however. The *process* of association is not merely mechanical or instinctive; it can develop in different kinds of ways, is adaptable, and provides a context of upbringing and learning that is sufficiently flexible to allow humans to cope with a wide variety of changing circumstances.

The culture developed through the mutual association of humans has, as essential components, morality, family life, work of some kind, recreation, and a form of religious or metaphysical outlook. It is in such contexts that people come to know what it is to be loved and valued and to know what it is to love and value other people. They acquire a sense of social identity and self-esteem through participation in their culture and community. The sense of belonging to some social grouping is a quite basic need for most people, and our particular values, opinions, knowledge, interests, and skills are developed through participation in such a grouping.

If this is right, attachment to a particular grouping is highly important to the individual and not given up easily. The point must be put in this tentative way because, in the first place, I am not concerned to introduce yet another deterministic account of social differentiation. Second, societies differ greatly in the scope they give individuals for moving away from their background and entering a new milieu, and it needs to be said that modern industrial and postindustrial societies, relative to other kinds of societies, allow a great deal of scope in this respect.

The attachment of a person to a social group and community with its attendant knowledge, skills, and values is not a light matter and cannot be ignored in any account of social class differences. If this point is anything near correct, most people remain in the social groupings that they belong to because that is where they wish to be and where they feel most at ease. Most individuals are not "upwardly mobile" but are proud of their communities, their upbringing, and their outlook. They feel similarly about their abilities and their interests. Any program of social reform, including mass education, ignores these facts about human beings at its peril.

Even those who make the transition to another range of possibilities through educational success, for example, feel an acute tension between one way of life and another. It is hardly surprising, therefore, that many do not wish to be placed in such a situation of conflict and discomfort. Here is a quotation from the English autobiographer, Edward Blishen, a boy from a lower-middle-class London background, describing his arrival at a grammar school (Queens) after winning a scholarship at elementary school, to help illuminate the general point from one person's point of view:

> It was not, this huge difference between elementary school and grammar school, any single item: it was a bewildering mass of them. It was the beginning of the social wrench that was to become more and more painful as time went on; the alienation from old friends, old quarters of the town . . . from our own parents. It was the scorn for the former furniture of our lives on which the existence of Queen's rested. (Blishen 1978, 89)

In concluding this chapter, I would like to make a few remarks about the relationship between abilities, knowledge, and interest. We have already seen that theories of intelligence try to isolate intellectual ability from other parts of the human mind and to look at it as a discrete entity. It can then be coupled with interest or skillful usage (cf. de Bono 1976) to provide an optimum performance. The ability one has is fixed, the best one can do is to ensure that it is well used.

Let us suppose for a moment that it is not possible to separate abilities from interests in such a neat way. Then the ability to do certain things and to acquire knowledge is not readily separable from motivation and interest. What is more, motivation and interest, when they are present, improve and develop ability in the activity in question. Motivation and interest, when they are present, sharpen and augment ability at an activity. Conversely, when there is little or no interest, ability remains generally low. Interests and abilities shaped in a particular way of life are indispensable to our understanding of what a person is capable of doing and how it is reasonable to expect him or her to develop. In this view, ability is not merely realized but also can be developed through the presence of motivation and interest. The possibility of acquiring insight, seeing important connections, working swiftly and skillfully, taking pains, and so on would, in this view, depend on the development of ability through a deepening of interest and motivation. A proper respect and attachment to a skill, discipline, or activity would then become an important condition of increasing one's ability.

The view of the development of ability just outlined has several features worth remarking at this stage. Ability is not a global attribute but is rather seen as "ability at" some particular activity connected with a particular contextual rationality. It is not sharply separable from interest and motivation but is seen as developing and being developed by them.

There is no natural limit to a person's abilities at an activity determined by intelligence or I.Q. Interest, motivation, and the perception of the significance of a task are connected with a cultural background and the characteristic preoccupations of that cultural background. As regards educational achievement, the involvement of literacy in certain activities peculiar to certain social groups is likely to evoke sustained application where it is perceived to be central to the interests and concerns of that group and where it enjoys some degree of prestige among that group.

CHAPTER 4

The theory of intelligence

The theory of intelligence and intelligence quotient (I.Q.) is based on four main assumptions. The first is that intelligence is a dispositional property of an individual independent of its exercise through particular activities. That is, one's intelligence is a tendency to perform under certain conditions, but the activities in which it is exercised do not themselves characterize one's intelligence, but one's intelligence helps to characterize one's performance of the activity (together with other factors such as motivation and interest). Intelligence can be seen as standing behind performance. I am not merely a more or less able mechanic, I am a more or less able mechanic depending on my general intelligence together with other factors. Indeed, it is claimed that my ability at *any* activity is determined by my intelligence and that my performance can be depressed by—for example—lack of interest (Vernon 1950, 112–13).

There are differences among I.Q. theorists as to what constitutes intelligence. Some, following Spearman, have claimed that it is a unitary attribute of mind. Others, like Burt, have described it as a hierarchical structure of general abilities from the lowest sensory-motor capacities upwards to memory and association, to imagination, verbal and arithmetical ability, practical and mechanical ability, and, finally, to the higher relational level of thought processes: apprehension of relations, combination of relations, and aesthetic processes (Burt 1949, 118–33). Jensen (1969) and Eysenck (1973) postulate level-1 and level-2 mental processes: the former are associative and the latter conceptual (Jensen 1969, 237–38).

Intelligence is a quality of the mind, independent of ability at particular activities. What, then, is its basis? There appear to be two views on this matter—one is that it is a theoretical construct out of correlations on various tests that has no physical existence (e.g., Eysenck 1973, 44, Nunnally 1981, chap. 10 and 13, for a detailed account of the factor-analytical techniques underlying intelligence specification). On the other hand, some I.Q. theorists tend to see intelligence as an attribute of the brain and nervous system (e.g., Burt 1955, 185–86).

Second, intelligence, all the major I.Q. theorists hold, has an upper limit. One may function below one's potential but never increase that potential. As Galton puts it, in an analogy with physical strength:

Everybody who has trained himself to physical exercises discovers the extent of his muscular powers to a nicety. When he begins to walk, to row, to use the dumb bells or to run, he finds to his great delight that his sinews strengthen, and his endurance of fatigue increases day after day. So long as he is a novice, he perhaps flatters himself that there is no assignable limit to the education of his muscles; but the daily gain is soon discovered to diminish, and at last it vanishes altogether. His maximum performance becomes a rigidly determinate quantity. He learns to an inch how high or how far he can jump, when he has attained the highest state of training. He learns to half a pound the force he can exert on the dynamometer, by compressing it. He can strike a blow against the machine used to measure impact, and drive the index to a certain graduation, but no further. So it is in running, in walking and in every other form of physical exertion. There is a definite limit to the muscular powers of every man, which he cannot by any education or exertion overpass.

This is precisely analogous to the experience that every student has had of the working of his mental powers. (Galton 1892, 25–26)

Third, intelligence is something definite; moreover, it is precisely quantifiable. Here is Eysenck, following Spearman in breaking down the nature of the mental operations involved in intelligence (at least, for Eysenck, of its higher features):

(1) A person has more or less power to apprehend outer reality and inner states of consciousness—apprehension.
(2) Whenever a person has in mind two or more ideas, he has more or less power to bring to mind any relations that essentially hold between them—education of relations.
(3) Whenever a person has in mind an idea together with a relation, he has more or less power to bring into mind the correlative idea—eduction of correlates (Eysenck 1973 p. 46, following Spearman 1927).

The I.Q. test, which gives a quantified assessment of the strength of these attributes, consists of three aspects of mental operation: speed, error checking, and persistence (Eysenck 1973, 62–63). The I.Q., which is measured by an I.Q. test, is a quantified amalgam of these three attributes of mental ability, which is in turn the operation of one or more of Spearman's three laws of apprehension, eduction of relations, and eduction of correlates. A measure of I.Q. is therefore a measure of speed, persistence, and error checking in the activities of apprehension and eduction of relations and correlates.

Not only is I.Q. said to be a fixed quantum of intellectual ability, but it can also be closely correlated with occupational status, in the sense outlined in Chapter 3. For normal, healthy people, I.Q. ranges over 50 points, from 90 to 140. Eysenck, condensing the results of various empirical studies, shows precisely how the mean I.Q. for a sample can be correlated with occupational status. On the left of Table 1.1 is the mean I.Q. of the occupational group measured.

In the theory of I.Q. we apparently have the answer to the question posed in Chapter 1 about the causes of different levels of educational achievement among the social classes. General intelligence or I.Q. determines educational achievement, which in turn determines occupational success. Kelley (1928, 78) points out that if Spearman is correct in thinking that education has little effect on general intelligence, then general scholastic achievement is little affected by education. Most I.Q. theorists would not draw such bleak conclusions as that. They would follow Eysenck in saying that I.Q. imposes a ceiling on educational achievement and that a high I.Q. score is a necessary but not a sufficient condition for high educational and occupational achievement. Those theorists who propose a hierarchical structure of mental faculties would also point to the necessity of different types or at least different emphases in the types of learning appropriate to people with high I.Q.s and people with low I.Q.s. Some theorists reject the "different types of mind" approach as put forward in the Norwood Report of 1943 (e.g., Vernon 1950), about which more in Chapter 5.

So far we have looked at three components of I.Q. theory. First, the view that intelligence is an attribute that underlies particular abilities rather than being a feature of a particular ability or group of abilities. Second, that intelligence has a definite upper limit to its quantity. Third,

Table 1.1

Mean I.Q. of Different Professional and Occupational Groups
(after Eysenck 1973)

140	Higher professional; top civil servants; professors and research scientists.
130	Lower professional; physicians and surgeons; lawyers; engineers (civil and mechanical).
120	Schoolteachers; pharmacists; accountants; nurses; stenographers; managers.
110	Foremen; clerks; telephone operators; salesmen; policemen; electricians; precision fitters.
100+	Machine operators; shopkeepers; butchers; welders; sheet-metal workers.
100−	Warehousemen; carpenters; cooks and bakers; small farmers; truck and van drivers.
90	Laborers; gardeners; upholsterers; farmhands; miners; factory packers and sorters.

that intelligence can be given a precise numerical quantity that reflects the interaction of mental speed in carrying out the basic operations, error checking, and persistence. It is now time to turn to what is perhaps the most controversial aspect of I.Q. theory—namely, its *hereditarian* claims.

I.Q. theorists claim that intelligence is a natural quality that is in large measure inherited from one's parents. This view is supported by statistical evidence that purports to show that seventy to eighty percent of a person's intelligence can be accounted for by genetic rather than environmental factors. This evidence comes from studies of correlations between parents and children and various twin or sibling studies (cf. Eysenck 1973, 102).

Here, then, seems to be a scientific justification for a Platonic model of society where the most able have, by a process of self-selection, assumed commanding and prestigious positions and, by genetically passing their natural ability to their offspring, perpetuate a castelike society layered occupationally in terms of intellectual ability (Herrnstein 1971). Not all I.Q. theorists draw this conclusion from the evidence. Eysenck (1973) in particular points to what he calls the factor of regression, that is, "the genetic factor which causes children of very bright and very dull parents to regress to the mean of the whole population" (Eysenck 1973, 219). He argues that Herrnstein underestimates the effects of regression and asserts, "Within a few generations, the differences in I.Q. between the children of very bright and very dull parents will have been completely wiped out" (Eysenck 1973, 219).

This point is, of course, quite consistent with the concept of a society structured in terms of its members' natural inherited ability, and in Chapter 1 we saw that Plato himself was careful to point out that silver parents could produce gold children and so on, and that the guardians should exercise a careful selection of children. What Herrnstein does is to make one's membership of a social class determined by inherited I.Q. rather than merely by one's potential for intellectual achievement determined by inherited I.Q.

Here are the four major components of I.Q. theory:

(1) I.Q. is a factor that *underlies* particular abilities.
(2) I.Q. is a fixed potential for intellectual achievement.
(3) I.Q. can be given a precise numerical value.
(4) I.Q. is to a large degree inherited by children from their parents.

How then is an I.Q. test administered? I.Q. tests are standardized sets of intellectual puzzles designed to establish, among other things, the strength of Spearman's eductive operations. These operations are examined in a variety of contexts: arithmetical, logical, linguistic, and perceptual. Tests that do not rely too heavily on home background (i.e., tests without a strong verbal or arithmetical component) are said to be "culture free," that is, they do not place people from relatively uneducated cultural backgrounds at a disadvantage.

The allegedly hierarchical character of intellectual ability has been probed in another way, notably by Jensen. Jensen observed that children of low socioeconomic status with low measured I.Q. often performed significantly better on tests that measured rote learning, trial-and-error learning, and free recall. Children of high socioeconomic status but low I.Q. did not do so well on these tests, their performance reflecting the performance they gave on the I.Q. tests (Jensen 1969).

To account for this discrepancy, Jensen postulated two types of mental process called level 1 and level 2. Level-1 processes correspond to the lower levels of Burt's structure of the mind; level-2 processes correspond to the higher levels. A good performance at level 1 is a necessary but not a sufficient condition for ability at level 2. Jensen proposes that the precise nature of the deficit of some children of low socioeconomic status is to be found in their lack of level-2 abilities.

To return to the I.Q. tests, they are administered individually or in groups. They involve the solution of abstract puzzles to which generally there is one correct solution. It should be noted that very often the tests are not deductions but rather exercises in analogical reasoning where the solution fits a preexisting pattern. A deduction is a form of argument that, if valid, specifies that given the truth of the premises, the conclusion must be allowed to be true (cf. Salmon 1963). Analogies are looser and more open to interpretation; it is only because the tester has nominated one "correct" answer that these patterns of reasoning *appear* like deductions.

Not all tests are, strictly speaking, tests for Spearman's eductions. For example, on the Stanford–Binet test, there are definitions, the copying of geometrical figures, memory tasks, number concepts, memory for stories, and comprehension and interpretation of proverbs (cf. Ginsberg 1972). Eysenck would, however, maintain that the essential nature of the mental processes involved always remains the same (Eysenck 1973, 46).

When they are computed, scores obtained on the test yield a measure called "mental age." This measure can be converted into intelligence quotient, or I.Q., by the following formula:

$$\text{I.Q.} = (\text{Mental Age} \div \text{Chronological Age}) \times 100.$$

Other formulas are now used more commonly, but the above gives a simple and easily understood example of the procedure. Whatever the procedure, the tests are constructed and calculated so that results in a given population have a certain distribution, called the "normal distribution," with the most frequent results occurring about the mean and with few extremely high or extremely low scores.

Here, then, is a very brief account of the theory and practice of I.Q. testing. One final point should be made about the administration of the test, whose importance will emerge in later chapters. The test may be administered individually or in groups, but, in order to make it fair, it is administered in identical conditions for the subjects with set routines for answering questions, time limits, number of probes, and so on. It is an unusual situation in many respects and one unlike the usual context of the exercise of most people's abilities.

CHAPTER 5

Intelligence quotient theory and education

Whether or not one takes the view that intelligence is a unitary factor of the mind or that it is a hierarchy of abilities, there are important implications for the way an educational system is conceived and run, and for the curriculum and teaching methods, should one adopt either of these two points of view.

The most important consequence of I.Q. theory for education is the view that intelligence is a fixed quantity. If I.Q. is fixed and can be measured, it follows that the most education can achieve is to ensure that children perform to the best of their ability as measured by the test. As I.Q. theorists, following Plato, generally take it for granted that the pursuit of knowledge for its own sake, and theoretical and aesthetic activities in general, are the most demanding areas of intellectual life, at the apex of a pyramid of intellectual activity, it also follows that a type of education usually associated with the grammar school (in the United Kingdom) is most appropriate for children who achieve the highest I.Q. scores.

Practical and technical activities of one sort or another require intellectual ability, but not of the degree of subtlety involved in the use of language. Instead, "uncanny insight into the intricacies of mechanism" (Norwood 1943) leave certain children needing a technical and practically oriented curriculum. Finally, there are those children whose interests are practical and who are not capable of thinking beyond the immediate environment or of relating different lines of study to one another. Such children may have pronounced ability in a particular technique such as rote memory or associative learning but, generally speaking, would not be able to command either the subtler aspects of language-related activities or the more intricate aspects of technical and practical skills.

Such a tripartite division of different kinds of minds is to be found in the Norwood Report of 1943. The recommendations of the Norwood Report helped to lay the foundations for a postwar system of secondary schooling in the United Kingdom based on grammar, technical, and secondary modern schools. Although clearly influenced by psychometrical theories about the hierarchical nature of intellectual ability, the Norwood Report did not, nonetheless, completely satisfy the I.Q. theorists. I.Q. theorists have been wary of too rigid a division of children into different mental types. As Vernon puts it:

The notion of types of people, as distinct from types of ability, should also be discouraged. As Burt . . . points out, there is no more justification for talking of an academic or practical type of child than for a tall or a short type. (Vernon 1950, 153)

What is important for I. Q. theory is the *rank ordering* of ability on a scale of I.Q. Types of activity are rank ordered through aesthetic and theoretical at the top of the scale, down through technical and practical activities, to domestic and manual activity at the bottom of the scale. The adoption by a child of one rather than another is due to the influence of motivation and interest but, above all, to ability rather than the possession of a different *kind* of mind. The higher-ability child is therefore *potentially* better at all activities than the lower ability child:

But if we could study the whole range of 15 year old pupils we should find that the grammar school pupils are usually superior to secondary modern pupils not only in mathematics, but also in football. (Vernon 1950, 113)

There are some differences between I.Q. theorists on this matter. For example, as we have seen, Jensen (1969) postulates two different kinds of thinking among different groups. Generally speaking, there is a tension between claims that differences in intelligence are a matter of *degree* and claims that they are a matter of *kind*, and the two claims are not easily reconciled with each other. I.Q. theorists' suspicions of the "Norwood Ideology" spring from that report's apparent rejection of the hierarchical view of intelligence. They also have other objections to Norwood, ones that bring out the educational implications of I.Q. theory with great clarity.

I.Q. theory holds that intellectual ability, as measured by the intelligence quotient, is fixed. Because it does not increase with age, and because it sets limits to the level of education attainable by an individual, the possibility of selection by test for level of education is very strong. The eleven-plus examination, which determined the type of secondary education a child would follow, was based on the notion that ability was (1) relatively unitary, (2) fixed, and (3) quantifiable.

Norwood was much more cautious in approach, stressing the developmental aspect of intellectual maturation. Intellectual aptitudes and tastes could be mistaken; it was not until about the age of thirteen that definite judgments should be made about what type of school a child should enter. The main methods of assessment were to be pupil records of progress put together by the teachers who had taught the child. Norwood was cautious about intelligence testing, regarding the test as supplementary to the pupil record and to be used in full consciousness of its experimental nature (Norwood 1943, 17):

Thus by the use of the records of the primary school together with subsidiary tests, and by a period of observation and trial in the lower school, differentiation would become a process, in which time and opportunity would be given for study of the relevant considerations, rather than a snap judgement dependent upon performance in an examination. (Norwood 1943, 18)

After the 1944 Education Act in Britain the following situation applied. The tripartite division of Norwood was put in place, but not the cautious, longitudinal assessment recommended by that report. Instead, the eleven-plus examination, with its bias towards theoretical, literacy-based achievements, became the major educational sieve through which grammar school pupils were selected. Grammar schools catered for academically minded pupils, technical schools for the technically minded and secondary modern schools catered for those who do not fit into the former two categories, that is pupils who did not have a very strong academic or technical vocation but whose interests were oriented largely to the environment in which they lived (Norwood 1943, 21). In practice, most children went to secondary modern schools, the technical schools failing to establish themselves to any significant extent.

The I.Q. testing movement contributed in a highly significant way to the system of secondary selection and education that operated in postwar Britain. I.Q. theorists have also sought to influence teaching methods, although with less success. We have already noted how Jensen distinguished between level-1 and level-2 cognitive abilities. Some level-1 abilities, connected with rote and associative learning, do not show any substantial between-group differences; level-2 abilities, which involve "self-initiated elaboration and transformation of the stimulus-input before it eventuates in overt response," did show significant social class differences (Jensen, cited in Eysenck 1973, 252).

Level-2 abilities are only well-developed in children with high "g" or general intelligence. Because modern discovery and child-centered educational methods require the exercise of level-2 abilities, the child with poor level-2 abilities is put at a disadvantage. According to this claim, we should recognize the diversity of distribution of intelligence within the community and plan curricula accordingly, rather than seeking to give all children a level-2 type curriculum, which is only really appropriate to a few.

To summarize, the implications of I.Q. theory for educational achievement are as follows. Potential educability is indicated by I.Q. test performance. Education may achieve but not go beyond that fixed potential. Because I.Q. is fixed at a relatively early age, a system of once-for-all selection based on intelligence and related tests is appropriate for the selection of children for different types of schooling. Discovery and exploration methods, which may well favor children with a high I.Q., are inappropriate for low-I.Q. children, for whom methods of instruction associated with drill, rote learning, and the building up of associations will be more appropriate.

CHAPTER 6

A critique of the theory of intelligence quotient

It is the contention of this chapter that the theory of an "intelligence quotient" is quite inadequate as an account of human ability. I do not wish to dwell too long on criticisms of I.Q. theory that have been made on empirical grounds, although these will be mentioned where they are relevant, but will concentrate instead on criticism of the philosophical assumptions underlying the theory.

The prime contention of I.Q. theory is that there exists a faculty of the mind, which could be called "intelligence," that determines our abilities in different forms of human activity. This faculty may or may not be seen as a structured hierarchy, but in either version it is seen as an underlying condition of the development of ability; in particular, it sets limits to individual potential in all fields of mental endeavor.

Galton's theory of a "ceiling" on intelligence was based on an analogy with physical strength. Try as hard as he might, the village blacksmith would find that certain feats of physical exertion could not be surpassed: "There is a definite limit to the muscular powers of every man, which he cannot by any education or exertion overpass." (Galton 1892, 26).

Galton saw intelligence just as he saw physical strength, a single quality of a person with definite limits. But it is misleading to look at physical strength, let alone mental ability, in this way. People are more or less good at different physical activities. A may be better at lifting than B, but less speedy. B may have stronger jaws but weaker lungs than A. Ryle puts this point well:

> Small boys, dreaming of athletic glory, are apt to ascribe all sporting prowess to "muscle." They have yet to learn: (1) that we have lots of muscles, so that A can have stronger biceps or thews but weaker jaw muscles than B; (2) that A may tug or hit more forcibly than B, yet may not last so well; (3) that A though weaker than B, may well exceed him in agility, lissomness, tenacity, balance, precision of movement, resilience, sure footedness, vigour, co-ordination, nerve, etc. Muscular powers are highly variegated in kind, as well as being indefinitely variable in degree; and any one of them can vary quite or nearly independently of all or most of the others. There is no safe inference from Hillary's mountaineering prowess to the loudness of his singing or to the speed of his sprinting. So there is no answer to the over-generic question How strong is he?, but at best, to some such specific questions as How strong is he at tree-felling? Even pretty specific questions are often

unanswerable like How strong is he at horse-riding? At boxing? (Ryle 1974, 53)

Ryle argues that intelligence, like strength, is not a single quantity, so that questions about degree of intellect can be asked only about ability in different activities. "How intelligent is he?" like "How strong is he?" is not a question that can receive a clear answer. I shall return to this point in more detail below, but first of all another aspect of Galton's strength analogy deserves mention. While it makes no sense to speak of the village blacksmith being infinitely strong, it does not follow that his best performance with the hammer to date in any way sets a limit to his future performance. His performance is difficult to beat not because it constitutes a record but because it was a difficult achievement. That a performance is a best performance to date does not constitute it as a ceiling of ability (cf. Ryle 1974, 53–54).

In a similar manner, we cannot establish a *ceiling* on intellectual ability by looking at best performance to date by an individual. He may not like the test conditions; he may lack interest in the subject; and practice and instruction in an activity may improve his performance. Whatever his performance might be at a particular activity that involves the application of the intellect, we are not entitled to make any safe inference about his general intellectual ability.

This is, of course, what intelligence testers claim that we are entitled to infer from performance on one particular sort of activity, namely, an intelligence test. It is worth looking again at the general ability that is measured in a test. Following Spearman, the nature of mental powers can be broken down into three components: (1) the ability to apprehend reality and states of consciousness; (2) the ability to bring to mind any relations that hold between two ideas; and (3) the ability to bring to mind a correlative idea when one has in mind one idea together with a relation.

What is in question is whether or not there are such *general* abilities as opposed to specific abilities at particular activities. A little investigation should reveal that there are not. What, for example, is the ability to apprehend reality? If this means something like "becoming aware of the world around us," then it is fairly clear that there is no such general ability. The phrase "to apprehend reality" suggests a fairly passive consciousness that receives data of varying strength through the sense organs, data that is then grasped and retained with varying degrees of tenacity.

But what people actually *do* is not like that at all. Consider various forms of "apprehending reality." A hunter examines traces of animals passing through a forest. A navigator looks at the stars, feels the wind and the swell of the waves. A wine merchant assesses the wine on his palate. A lawyer examines a brief. A churchgoer takes part in Holy Communion. The list could go on indefinitely, but we will not get any clearer as to what "apprehending reality" is, for there is no such general ability. The ways in which people become aware of the world are highly specific and depend not only on perceptions that have been trained, but also on the emphasis and value that are put on certain phenomena by the activity concerned or by the culture to which the individual belongs, as well as on his or her interest, motivation, and past experience.

The way in which a football referee "apprehends reality," for example, will depend on his general knowledge of the game and its rules, informal conventions that also govern play, his knowledge of individual players, the way in which he has trained his perception to notice what is going on in the field of play, and on many other factors besides. If there is no such general faculty as "apprehending reality," are there such faculties as eduction of ideas and correlates, considered in a general way? The way in which two objects or two ideas (it is not clear what I.Q. theorists mean by ideas, but they probably include perceptions) are related can be realized in many different ways as well as by many different relations. As a model of the activity of the mind, it is highly unconvincing.

People wish to gain information about various matters, to perform various tasks, *and* to relax and converse with other people. In what sense does all this activity involve the eduction of ideas and correlates? Mental activity can sometimes involve something like this, perhaps in artificial situations like a game, a puzzle, or a test. This model of intellectual activity works best when two or more clear ideas are presented and someone is invited to guess or in some way work out a relationship between them. In these cases there is invariably just one "correct" answer because the permissible alternatives are enumerated. For example:

"High is to low as Big is to: small, large, down, fair. (Underline correct answer)." (Eysenck 1973, 47)

But this model applies only in very restricted situations in human life, and these turn out to be similar to those in which tests like I.Q. tests are carried out. The whole question as to what general intelligence is and whether or not it can be measured is thereby begged.

The Spearman account of mental activity derives from British empiricist philosophy, notably from the work of John Locke. Locke's account of reasoning depends on the association in the mind of different ideas. His account of the acquisition of ideas depends on a theory of knowledge that involves the imprinting of sensations on our minds and of the internal operation of the mind on those sensations (Locke 1961, 2:77–78). Mental activity is seen as something distinct from activity in the external world such as what we would normally call human actions. The work of the mind is separated conceptually from the work of the body. It is natural, then, if one accepts this model of the mind, to think that intellectual activity can be reduced to a small number of mental operations.

One difficulty with such an account is that it accords badly with our everyday descriptions of the exercise of intellectual ability that relate to our performance of an enormous variety of different sorts of actions. Most human activity is practical in nature—that is, it is directed toward the furtherance of projects, tasks, customs, rituals, and the maintenance of social and material life. Our understanding of the nature of the rationality involved in the activity is dependent on our understanding of the nature of the activity itself. The rational activity of a person cannot be reduced to the Spearman principles. Consider for example, the contextual rationality involved in navigation by a Trukese navigator, which Gladwin (1964) goes on to compare to the work of a European navigator:

> Essentially the Trukese navigator relies on dead reckoning. He sets his course by the rising and setting of stars, having memorised for this purpose the knowledge gleaned from generations of observations of the direction in which stars rise and fall through the seasons. A heading toward a given island, is set for a particular season a trifle to the left, or perhaps the right, of a certain star at its setting or rising. Through the night a succession of such stars will rise or fall, and each will be noted and the course checked. Between stars, or when the stars are not visible due to daylight or storm, the course is held constant by noting the direction of the wind and the waves. A good navigator can tell by observing wave patterns when the wind is shifting its direction and speed, and by how much. In a dark and starless night the navigator can even tell these things from the sound of the waves as they lap upon the side of the canoe's hull, and the feel of the boat as it travels through the water. All of these complex perceptions—visual, auditory, kinaesthetic—are combined with vast amounts of data stored in memory, and the whole is integrated into a slight increase or decrease in pressure on the steering paddle, or a grunted instruction to slack off the sail a trifle. (Gladwin 1964, 111–12).

Gladwin points out the similarity in some respects of the actions, perceptions, of the experienced motorist on a busy road. Contrasted with the Trukese is the European navigator:

> The cognitive strategy of the European navigator can be characterised as essentially deductive, proceeding from principles to details. Before he embarks on a voyage, or upon a new course, he takes into account a number of factors, both general and specific, which will govern his subsequent actions. These may include the organisation of his vessel, policies of his organisation, the urgency of his cargo, probable weather conditions and appropriate time for arrival at his destination. Out of the possible conflicting mandates flowing from these considerations he will develop a plan which will incorporate compromises but will constitute his organizing principle of operation. In implementing this plan he will again be governed by navigational and other techniques which are concrete applications of basic principles. Some of these, such as the movement of celestial bodies, are highly abstract in nature and are translatable into a navigational fix only through several steps of deductive

logic. The navigator may or may not understand all the theory which lies behind his techniques, but they had originally to be developed through an explicit sequence of logical steps. However, once the European navigator has developed his operating plan and has available the appropriate technical resources, the implementation and monitoring of his navigation can be accomplished with a minimum of thought. (Gladwin 1964, 117)

Another good example of the distinctive intellectual character of a certain practical activity is one discussed by MacMillan (1982). The wheelwright's trade was one that depended heavily on the acquisition of experience, not just of the business of measurement and working with wood, but also of the soil and the trees of the locality and the requirements of individual customers, experience that was in turn based partly on knowledge of the surrounding land and farms. MacMillan points out that very often the application of scientific techniques and theoretical knowledge is quite inappropriate to excellence at this sort of activity (cf. MacMillan 1982, 48–52).

I do not wish to suggest that there is no common thread to rational activities, that there are not certain general features of our constitutive rationality (see Chapter 2), but this is very far from reducing all rational activity to Spearman's three operations. It is interesting that I.Q. testing relates most naturally to those sorts of activities that are relatively passive, contemplative, and not particularly related to practical considerations, and that also, to a large degree, depend on some theoretical, formal knowledge of language (cf. Ginsberg 1972, Hirsch 1989).

A high valuation of this kind of contemplative, theoretical, and relatively abstract kind of intellectual activity is one that is deeply ingrained in Western culture and is particularly ingrained in academic life and in the education systems of Western countries (some more than others). Like Plato, there is a tendency among the ruling and educational elites to value theory, contemplation, and nonpractical research among the highest forms of human activity. Their very "uselessness" is often cited as a sign of their unconditional value, particularly in the United Kingdom. Such activities, also seen as most taxing to the human mind, are also naturally seen to bring out most clearly that quality of the human mind known as intelligence.

It is not part of my business, at the moment, to question the value that our culture places on certain types of rationality. I merely wish to point out that whatever value is placed on theoretical rationality, concentration on it as a paradigm of human intellectual activity will tend to channel our vision away from other manifestations of the working of the human mind. If we move away from the model of the human mind suggested by I.Q. theory and pay more attention to human activity in its context, then the influence of motivation and interest become clearer as well. Galton's idea of a ceiling on performance has been seen to be misleading.

The separation of intellect from interest and motivation as a distinct feature of the mind reinforces the idea of an "intellectual ceiling." When intellectual activity is seen in a practical and cultural context, as it should be, then the importance of these factors becomes much clearer.

Excellence, where it depends on practice, experience, learning by example, and background knowledge, will thrive on a strong degree of interest and commitment. Interest in an activity will lead to more practice, more knowledge, and greater understanding. So will a strong desire to do well. Very often, immersion in the technique of an activity, say football or a trade like motor-vehicle repair, involves participation in a culture and social milieu in which knowledge, technique, and skills are passed on indirectly in the course of social and leisure activities. In this way, being part of a certain cultural milieu enhances commitment and hence performance. The development of ability depends to a striking extent on social and human development within one's culture.

These points help to illuminate Eysenck's account of what features of mental performance are being measured in an I.Q. test. The test, as we saw, is thought to measure three aspects of mental performance: speed, persistence, and error checking. The last two factors are particularly related to interest and commitment. One is more likely to persevere and to take care when one has a strong desire to do well in an activity than when such a desire is absent. What is more, because these two factors are related to interest and commitment, they are likely to be brought out and developed in different activities rather than to be present as general factors in all activities. It is particularly implausible to suggest that someone whose background does not lead him to value a formal education particularly highly is likely to show the same degree of persistence and error checking in the performance of an I.Q. test as someone whose background leads him to value education and has a strong desire to do well in tests. It is even more implausible to suggest that these are fixed quantities due largely to hereditary factors when their relationship and interaction with other aspects of the personality and with a person's social and cultural context are so intimate.

This leaves mental speed as the important feature of the intellect measured by an I.Q. test. If I.Q. is ultimately seen as a measure of speed in working out a relationship between ideas or an idea given a relation and another idea in a test situation or a puzzle where success depends on getting the right answer as determined by the test designer, then it is a poor thing indeed. Once again, when our attention moves away from tests and puzzles and we try to take in at least some of the vast variety of situations in which human abilities are exercised, then the inadequacy or inappropriateness of *speed* as a way to characterize excellence in them become obvious. Such virtues as mulling over a problem, "sleeping on it," trial-and-error methods, painstaking care, the consideration of alternatives, or the working out of different approaches to a problem are very often highly important. The I.Q. test has no place for the working out of alternatives, for original solutions, or for such mental features as aesthetic awareness and appreciation, features that are intimately related to imagination, the training of perception, and, in some cases, the development of certain physical skills—as, for example, in musicianship, painting, or sculpture.

Even where speed is an important feature of excellence in an activity, it is speed at *doing something* that is important, not just generalized speed in mental operation. Here one can make all sorts of contrast. Speed at working out a calculation is one example where there is a fixed solution and a minimum of physical activity involved. This is close to the I.Q. paradigm. Compare this with a footballer sizing up the situation on the field, a politician engaged in a television debate, or a singer learning a new aria. It would be absurd to describe the position of a general who is engaged in a series of strategic maneuvers and considering his next move to be searching for a single solution selected in advance by someone else. Although he may have to make a swift decision, it is in many ways unlike working out the solution to a test puzzle. For example, he may need to consider the position of his opponent, his personality and inclinations, the state of his army, the overall political situation in his opponent's country, the state of the weather, the surrounding terrain and communications, and a host of other matters. In such a situation what is going to serve him well is not just general speed, whatever that may be, but psychological and political insight, organizational ability, a wealth of previous experience gained from past campaigns, knowledge of weather and local geography and history, and an ability to listen to and consider advice and information, perhaps received through clandestine and possibly suspect channels.

Speed of decision making in one kind of activity is not necessarily appropriate to another kind of activity. This point is well made by the Duke of Wellington in his reported comments after chairing his first cabinet meeting as prime minister:

> "An extraordinary affair. I gave them their orders and they insisted on discussing them."

Speed is also related to practice, experience, and interest, even in activities like calculation, chess, and the solution of puzzles. There is no such thing as generalized mental speed independent of particular activities. I.Q. theorists are in pursuit of a chimera in looking for such a thing.

I.Q. and Educational Achievement

We have seen in Chapter 5 how I.Q. theory has affected educational policy in the past. I now want to look briefly at the implications of the theory for educational achievement in the light of the critique that has been developed of it. I.Q. theorists would cite social stratification and different levels of educational achievement and their correlation with I.Q. scores as evidence for the usefulness of I.Q. tests as measures of ability, and also as partial evidence for the hereditary nature of intelligence. What has the account given in this chapter got to say about these claims?

It is fairly clear that I.Q. tests measure something that is correlated with social and educational attainment. For someone to perform well on an I.Q. test, a literate and cultured home background is helpful. Even tests that are said to be "culture fair"—that is, that do not discriminate between different cultural backgrounds in terms of, for example, knowledge of vocabulary—presuppose a certain formal and theoretical attitude to language, or an acquaintance with certain kinds of games, toys, and puzzles. The tests also work with fairly limited and abstract forms of reasoning, which are the kinds of reasoning that the education system places a high value on, as do occupations concerned with the processing and the creative use of literary materials.

If we add to these considerations factors such as interest, motivation, and desire for social and educational success, which will, on the whole, be distributed differently among the different social classes (see Chapter 3), then the differences that are found between social groups on the tests are perhaps not all that surprising. It should also be noted that these are not *absolute* differences: scores are achieved on a continuous range, and there is an overlap between occupations in terms of individual scores. Eysenck's table, which we included in Chapter 4, shows *mean* scores for the different social groups.

What is worrying about such tests, particularly when they are relied on heavily, to the detriment of other methods of evaluation such as pupil profiles, is that they concentrate on such a narrow band of the spectrum of human intellectual activity. There is a danger, which has been realized in the past, that children will be labeled "low I.Q." and conveniently pigeonholed as nonacademic without any real effort being made to discover their true strengths or potential interests.

There is another real danger present in the use of these materials in an indiscriminate fashion. Quite apart from the I.Q. theory's dubious claim to be able to preselect academically able individuals, the I.Q. ideology implies that the high-I.Q. and hence academically able pupils are potentially better at *everything* than nonacademic pupils. This view is a dangerous one because it discourages attempts to provide an excellent education for those who are not academically inclined. We have already seen how Eysenck would favor rote-learning methods for those with low I.Q.s. What is really needed for nonacademic pupils are practical and stimulating programs that will engage the aptitudes and interests of those who do not wish—or are not able—to pursue academic studies.

A further pernicious effect of this "pigeonholing" is that I.Q. theory assumes that one's abilities do not change, that they are fixed at an early age. As most of us know, from knowledge either of ourselves or of other people, this is not true. As a child matures, his or her abilities and interests may develop in different ways, ways that could not have been predicted at an early age. There is great potential for waste in such a system, particularly when—as we have seen—there are good grounds for doubting its truth.

What of the claim of I.Q. theory that ability is largely inherited rather than acquired? One point we may note at this stage is that for our purposes all this claim amounts to is: "To what extent is the ability to perform on I.Q. tests inherited rather than acquired?" The question is put in this way because the argument so far has been that there is no such thing as general intellectual ability that can be readily quantified on a test.

The claim that this ability is largely inherited rather than acquired is largely a technical empirical one in the disciplines of genetics and statistics. The issue has been complicated by the alleged discovery of fraud in the work of Burt, who conducted what was supposed to be one of the most important studies of monozygotic twins reared apart in different social circumstances. There are those who argue that the invalidity of Burt's data casts doubt on the statistical validity of the remaining sample of monozygotic twin studies; others dispute this (cf. Blum 1980, Vroon 1980). Kleinig however, has argued, following Block and Dworkin, that it is not possible to measure inherited I.Q. independently of environmental influences. Differences in genetic make-up may themselves influence the response of the environment towards an individual. So, for example, a child who shows early evidence of high I.Q. might well affect the behavior of other persons towards him in such a way that performance in I.Q. tests is increased. Conversely, a child who shows evidence of low I.Q. may affect the behavior and attitudes of others in such a way as to retard performance on measures of I.Q. The methods used to assess the heritability of I.Q. count any variance produced by genetic variation as if it were genetically caused variance, even if it is also environmentally caused (Kleinig 1982, Chapter 11; Block and Dworkin 1977).

CHAPTER 7

Theories of cultural and verbal deficit

Psychometrically based theories of ability and educational achievement give us one view of how society is organized into classes on the basis of natural, inherited, general intellectual ability. Theories of cultural and verbal deficit focus on the culture and language of different social groups and the way in which this affects their education. Some groups are said to be "culturally deprived" in relation to other groups. This means that the knowledge they have, their means of gaining it, and their means of expressing it are inferior in comparison with other groups. This, in turn, drastically affects their ability to benefit from a formal education.

Appreciation of the importance of language is fundamental to the understanding of human societies, and it is not surprising to find that views on language and language use, and on their relation to different social groups, play a vital part in theories of cultural deprivation. One can go further and say that theories of language deficit are a subspecies and even form the core of these theories. Language deficit theories maintain that poor language and poor social conditions go together and that poor language, especially, is responsible for poor educational achievement. What "poor" means in this context is different from its meaning in the phrase "financially poor," although there would be, in most versions of the theories, an empirical association between the two types of poverty. Linguistic poverty is above all, a poverty in *what* can be talked about and *how* it can be expressed.

It is not surprising, either, to find that these theories are associated with a "different types of mind" view, which we found in Plato's picture of human nature. In fact, I.Q. theory and verbal- or linguistic-deficit theories have a close but variable relationship. Verbal-deficit theories place great importance on language rather than on tests without an obvious linguistic content. They have, however, tended to rely heavily on testing and quantitative measurement as a means of assessment. What is more, they are often *compatible* with I.Q. theory. That is, it is perfectly possible for verbal deficit and low I.Q. *jointly* to explain low educational achievement. An explanation of why someone with a high I.Q. does badly at school may rely on verbal-deficit theory and refer to a poor linguistic and cultural background.

We have already seen that I.Q. tests often have a significant, if not immediately obvious, verbal element in them. It is worth remarking, however, that even where this verbal element is not obvious, as in the question "High is to low as Big is to . . . ?" (quoted in Chapter 6), where a process of reasoning, even implicit reasoning, is required in order to arrive at an answer, then language plays a part, because reasoning is a verbal matter or, when done silently and implicitly, can at least in principle be put into words.

The obvious objection to this point is that those who are deaf or hard of hearing do not seem to be impaired in their performance on nonverbal I.Q. tests (cf. Jensen 1973, 285–87). Jensen appears to take the view that language does not have a general, decisive, or direct influence on intellectual development (cf. Furth 1961, 386–89). It is worth dwelling on this argument because it raises an important point, one that not only reverberates through the controversy over verbal-deficit theories but also touches on the debate over I.Q. theory. In an experiment by Furth (1961), deaf subjects had to understand a task presented to them—that is, they had to grasp *through language* what was required of them. The tasks on which deaf people performed at the same level as nondeaf people involved the recognition of sameness and symmetry, tasks that in themselves do not require linguistic ability. They performed less well than the hearing subjects on tests of opposition, acquisition and transfer, which involve a well-developed vocabulary (cf. also Furth 1973). Interesting as these results are, they hardly justify Furth's general conclusion that "language experience may increase the efficiency of concept formation in a certain situation, but is not a necessary prerequisite for the development of the basic capacity to abstract and generalize" (Furth 1961, 369).

Arguments such as this show a refusal to distinguish between different levels of language. We have already noted in Chapter 2 that all known human languages have the same structure for expressing roughly the same range of thought about the world. In particular, the logical operators such as "not . . . ," "all . . . ," etc., give every language a common basic apparatus for the expression of constitutive rationality. This point needs to be developed with great care. One can work from a metaphor that likens the logical structure of a language to the human skeleton, on the one hand, and the semantic fields and vocabulary of different contextual rationalities to the tissues of the body that depend on the skeleton for support, on the other.

Although this analogy is suggestive in pointing out certain fundamental features that all known human languages seem to have in common, it can also mislead because any attempt to demarcate the logical from the contextual parts of language in too neat a way can lead to difficulty. Logical inferences that depend on the sense of nonlogical terms in the premises are possible, and very often formal calculi fail to capture the full richness of the inferential possibilities of logical words (cf. Blackburn 1984).

Nevertheless, even when these qualifications have been made, the point still holds that a great deal of the fundamental logical structure of any language exists quite independently of the vocabulary of particular contextual rationalities. Furthermore, such structure gives us the core of constitutive rationality for any society, whatever its state of development. This is not to say that there will not often be fundamental differences between the contextual rationalities that may be available in a given society. For example, a people unaccustomed to games of chance such as those that involve the use of dice, coins, or cards will tend not to have highly developed notions of the quantitative measurement and calculation of probability (I am indebted to Dr. R. C. Solomon for this example).

Much of this core of rationality can be expressed in the formal systems known as propositional and predicate calculus (cf. Lemmon 1965, for an introductory account). In order to reason in such a language, no vocabulary apart from the logical operators is needed, just dummy symbols to represent sentences and predicates.

Now, it is perfectly possible to carry out a great deal of complex reasoning with a very limited vocabulary, provided that the relevant terms for expressing logical or analogical connections are understood. This situation applies to tests such as Raven's matrices, where correlates or relations are "educed" by choosing the right item from a number of alternatives. All that is required is that in principle a reason can be given for a choice according to a principle, rather than at random, for the testee to demonstrate that he or she is doing more than guessing the answers. There is no reason to suppose that a deaf person is in principle incapable of taking such steps of reasoning and justification.

What Jensen fails to notice is that languages for the deaf do exist. Their medium is visual, like the literary medium (although lacking its permanence), and it expresses the same degree of constitutive rationality as do spoken and written forms of language (cf. Menyuk 1988, 61–62). It is, of course, not surprising that the vocabulary of deaf people should develop at a slower rate than that of people with normal hearing, and therefore it is not surprising that they should score relatively poorly on verbal tests. It does not follow from these facts that intellectual development is primarily nonlinguistic in character. It is interesting to note, in this connection, that Basil Bernstein, a prominent verbal-deficit theorist whose views will be considered below, refers to a "nonverbal" test such as Raven's Progressive Matrices as a test of "non-linguistic relational problems involving logical addition and subtraction," as if such problems were nonlinguistic in character (cf. Bernstein 1958, 53).

Verbal-deficit theories share with I.Q. theory a view of society based on an intellectual hierarchy, one tending, if anything, to emphasize even more than would most I.Q. theorists the different *types* of cognition available to different social groups. In some versions there is also a strong *deterministic* element to the theory. That is, one's mode of speech and corresponding way of life are beyond the control of the individual, but are shaped for him by his family, upbringing, and social environment. Edwards (1974) complains of the "Frankenstein's monster" aspect of Bernstein's early work, and there is some justice to this complaint, as we shall see. The similarity with I.Q. theory in this respect is that one's I.Q. is largely shaped by genetic heritage and is thus beyond personal control.

Verbal-deficit theories, however, ascribe verbal deficit and its consequences to a person's social and cultural heritage, rather than to his or her genetic heritage, and this is a most significant difference. A social environment can be changed by human activity, whereas there is no known way of manipulating one's genes in order to increase the I.Q. of one's offspring. This feature of verbal-deficit theories—namely, the view that a change in linguistic behavior is in principle possible through a change in the linguistic, social, and educational environment—gives these theories a slant toward a more Rousseauist view of educational achievement. For if linguistic inequality is a social product, it can be changed by social action.

I.Q. theorists would reject the view that low intelligence is caused by verbal deficit because this would conflict with their view that low I.Q. has genetic rather than social origins (cf. Jensen 1973, 277–87). They take the view that verbal deficit is a by-product of low intelligence rather than vice versa. In its most Rousseauist form, verbal-deficit theories make the deficit little more than a difference in ways of thinking and speaking that happen to be valued differently by society and that give access to different levels of opportunity (e.g., Bernstein 1972, 225).

This apparent flexibility in verbal-deficit theories, in comparison with the rigid view of I.Q. theory that one's intellectual destiny is charted from birth, has made it seem in many ways a more attractive sort of explanation for low educational achievement than I.Q. theory. There is another feature of the verbal-deficit view that makes it attractive— namely, its apparent intuitive plausibility. It seems to many people that the obvious differences in the way that people from different social classes speak must have something very seriously to do with their social and educational position in life. But there is a great danger of confusion here. Verbal-deficit theorists are often at great pains to say that they are not concerned with *dialect* or *style* but with more fundamental patterns of speaking and thinking. Variation in *dialect* means differences in language according to time, geographical region, or social class. These differences show up in syntax (rules for combining words into sentences) and in vocabulary (the "dictionary" of the language). Differences in dialect, especially in societies that are culturally homogenous, are not so great as to pose serious barriers to understanding between different social groups and regions, although they can, on occasion, lead to difficulties. *Style* in speech refers either to the degree of formality that exists through occasion (compare a job interview with a chat in a bar or pub) or to the degree of respect shown by a speaker towards his or her audience. Dialect and style refer to *how* something is said rather than to *what* is said. For example,

"You don't ger' owt for nowt"

is another way of saying

"You don't get something for nothing."

Dialect and style are not, in themselves, fundamental variations in language of the sort that this book is interested in. Why is this so? For various reasons, some dialects may not have in their vocabulary words associated with certain activities. For example, technical terms associated with merchant banking are not likely to be in much use in the Barnsley area of South Yorkshire. But this sort of difference does not affect what was described in Chapter 2 as the *constitutive rationality* of the English language, of which Barnsley dialect and Standard English are but two variations. It means simply that they share a common capacity for reasoning and thinking about the world, differing in the ways in which that thinking and reasoning are expressed.

However, in social terms, different dialects and styles have different levels of *prestige*: they are valued differently in different parts of society. It is certainly true that in different situations different styles and dialects are more advantageous than others in both social and career terms. Dialect and style contribute powerfully to the sense of culture and community that, as I suggested in Chapter 3, is so important to a human sense of identity and well-being. To be "one of our own" is no small thing at any level of society, and ways of speaking convey a strong signal of belonging or not belonging to a particular group.

Probably the best way to get acquainted with verbal-deficit theories is to look at the work of Basil Bernstein, who is probably their best-known exponent. Bernstein's views, like those of I.Q. theorists, have aroused a lot of controversy. In Bernstein's case the controversy has been heightened by confusion over what he and his associates have actually meant by what they have said and written. How this confusion has arisen will emerge when we examine the development of his views. There are some commentators who strongly deny that Bernstein is or ever has been a deficit theorist (e.g., Atkinson 1985); as I hope to show, however, the evidence of Bernstein's own writings gives little support to this view.

Bernstein's earliest work (reported in Bernstein 1958) examined a group of sixteen-year-old working-class boys with two tests. One was

the Raven's Progressive Matrices (Raven 1938), the other was the Mill
Hill Vocabulary Scale (cf. Raven 1965). The tests are to be used together
and are in fact part of the equipment of I.Q. testing. The matrices are
a "nonverbal" test of reasoning by the completion of progressively more
difficult patterns of visual items; the Mill Hill test is a graded test of
knowledge of the meanings of English words. Raven notes that

> while the Matrices test provides a reliable index of a person's present capacity
> for intellectual activity whatever language he speaks or education he has
> acquired, the Mill Hill Vocabulary Scale provides a reliable index of the best
> intellectual level a person has attained whatever his present capacity for
> intellectual activity may happen to be. (Raven 1965, 1)

In other words, the two tests, when taken together, can be used to
compare actual and potential achievement. Bernstein found that the
higher I.Q. scores (measured by Raven's Matrices) were not matched
by high scores on the Mill Hill test:

> The clustering of the vocabulary scores about the mean, independent of
> matrices score, indicates the discrepancy between the ability to solve certain
> non-linguistic *relational* problems involving logical addition and subtraction,
> and purely linguistic problems of a conceptual or categorizing order. (Bern-
> stein 1958, 53)

I wish to comment later on exactly *what* is measured by these two
tests. For the present we can note that Bernstein concluded from this, and
from a later experiment that involved inter-class comparisons (Bernstein
1960), that a high I.Q. score did not necessarily mean that one's potential
was being fulfilled:

> It is suggested that the measurable interstatus differences in language facility
> result from entirely different *modes* of speech found within the middle class
> and the lower working class. The role intelligence plays is to enable the
> speaker to exploit more successfully the possibilities symbolized by the
> socially determined forms of language use. (Bernstein 1960, 78)

In Bernstein's view, therefore, it is the culture of the lower working
class that depresses linguistic performance irrespective of measured I.Q.
Note here that Bernstein is not rejecting I.Q. theory but building verbal-
deficit theory on it, although he does at one point suggest that general
intelligence may well be a matter of learning, thus parting company with
I.Q. theory on the heritability thesis (Bernstein 1960, 84).

What then is the nature of this deficit? Bernstein does not identify
linguistic modes—or what he later called elaborated and restricted
codes—with dialects. But it is clear that there is an empirical association
between low-prestige dialects and the restricted code. The restricted

code is a form of language (later it becomes a sort of mechanism that controls language) that limits the expression of rationality by its speakers. The elaborated code, on the other hand,is a suitable vehicle for the expression of rationality.

The "public language" (Bernstein's earlier term) or "restricted code" has a simple, even "poor" syntax, is only capable to making crude and simple logical distinctions, and has a limited vocabulary. Its users find it difficult to make their statements explicit and to present a reasoned point of view (Bernstein 1958, 66). It is clear that Bernstein was developing the idea that the restricted-code user has a different level of constitutive rationality (see Chapter 2) from that of the elaborated-code user. The simple, broken syntax and absence of all but a few logical operators, together with the inability of speakers to develop reasons for their statements, all ensure that this is so:

> Because of a simple sentence construction and the fact that a *public* language does not depend on the use of conjunctions—which serve as important logical distributors of meaning and sequence—a public language will be one in which logical modification and stress can only be rendered crudely linguistically. (Bernstein 1961a, 299)

The difference in the levels of constitutive rationality between the two codes is so great that there may even be difficulties in translating a logically complex language into a simpler one:

> The working class child has to translate and thus *mediate* middle class language structure through the logically simpler language structure of his own class in order to make it personally meaningful. Where he cannot make this translation he fails to understand and is left puzzled. (Bernstein 1958, 47)

The elaborated code, the vehicle of middle-class communication, is, by contrast, fully capable of a higher level of constitutive rationality, through its greater logical complexity. It has a larger and more differentiated vocabulary, and its users are accustomed to presenting and listening to reasoned arguments in support of views. The elaborated code allows the speaker to refer beyond the immediate context—spatial and temporal—and to talk about abstract rather than immediate, sensorily available matters.

The restricted-code user is bound by his location, his culture, and his community. His language does not allow him to think himself out of it. Even given his limited linguistic resources, he does not make good use of them as tools for reasoning: "Meanings are strung together like beads on a frame rather than following a logical sequence" (Bernstein 1959, 284).

The two codes also have consequences for the development of practi-

cal rationality. Concepts of causality and process will be poorly understood by the restricted-code user. Planning—i.e., the setting up and
carrying out of projects—given the context-bound nature of the thinking,
will not be possible. The restricted-code user is bound, by the way in
which he thinks and talks about the world, to the spatial and temporal
present. The sort of culture that gives rise to such patterns of speech and
thought is described by Bernstein thus:

> If a social group by virtue of its class relation, that is as a result of its common
> occupational and social status, has developed strong communal bonds; if the
> work relations of this group offer little variety or little exercise in decision
> making; if assertion, if it is to be successful, must be a collective rather than
> an individual act; if the work requires physical manipulation and control; if
> the diminished authority of the man at work is transformed into an authority
> of power at home; if the home is over-crowded and limits the variety of
> situations it can offer; if the children socialize each other in an environment
> offering little intellectual stimuli; if all these attributes are found in one setting,
> then it is plausible to assume that such a social setting will generate a particular
> form of communication which will shape the intellectual, social and affective
> orientation of the children. (Bernstein 1971, 165)

The elaborated code develops under the contrary sort of conditions.
Communal bonds are not so strong, work involves responsibility, decision making, and what Bernstein calls "symbolic organization and control." Home life is comfortable and affords intellectual stimulation for
the children. Here is an example of the conditions under which the
elaborated code will be employed:

> Imagine a husband and wife have just come out of the cinema, and are talking
> about the film. "What do you think?" "It had a lot to say." "Yes, I thought
> so too—let's go to the Millers, there may be something going on there." They
> arrive at the Millers, who ask about the film. An hour is spent on the
> complex, moral, political, aesthetic subtleties of the film and its place in the
> contemporary scene. Here we have an elaborated variant; the meanings now
> have to be made public to others who have not seen the film. The speech
> shows careful editing, at both the grammatical and lexical levels. It is no
> longer context-tied. The meanings are explicit, elaborated and individualized.
> While expressive channels are clearly relevant, the burden of meaning inheres
> predominantly in the verbal channel. The experience of the listeners cannot
> be taken for granted. Thus each member of the group is on his own as he
> offers his interpretation. (Bernstein 1973c, 201–2)

There is no doubt that at least in his earlier writings on the subject,
Bernstein paints a picture that involves some stark contrasts and, as far
as the restricted code goes, a pretty bleak vista. An impoverished social
background implies impoverished linguistic and intellectual resources.
The form of language use is said to be socially determined, and in some

respects the life that sustains it can be said to be barely a human kind of life at all. There is little scope for the exercise of rationality in the life of the restricted-code user; not only does he operate within a low level of constitutive rationality, determined by the logical simplicity of his language, but even within this he is unable to do much in the way of constructing reasoned arguments. Furthermore, he has difficulty in understanding causality and process and is unable to make rational plans for the future. He is locked into a world of the immediate here and now (cf. Bernstein 1958, 53–54).

It is useful to compare this description of working-class life with the way in which Marx distinguishes human life from that of animals. According to Marx, it is the ability to plan and to put plans into effect that marks our distinctive nature, and this ability is, in turn, intimately bound up with our use of language (cf. Marx 1887, 1:178; Marx 1858, 87–88; Rubinstein 1981).

What further evidence did Bernstein give for his views? There are a few surveys and experiments of his own and a great many by his associates. Bernstein (1960) reports an inter-class comparison of performance on the Matrices and Mill Hill tests, in which the working-class group, when matched with the middle-class group for performance on the Matrices test, did significantly worse on the Mill Hill vocabulary test. Bernstein (1962a) reports longer pauses between speech for middle-class than working-class adolescents, which was held to indicate speech planned less well on the part of the working class. Bernstein (1962b) reports on the same group of people as was used in 1960 and 1962a, and notes that there are significant differences between middle-class and working-class groups in the use of various grammatical constructions such as the passive, and in the use of uncommon adjectives, adverbs, and conjunctions. The middle-class group used more of these and also more of what Bernstein calls "egocentric sequences" such as "I mean" and "I think." Finally, in a piece of research by Hawkins (1969), one often cited by Bernstein, two groups of seven-year-old children—one working-class, the other middle-class—were shown a simple story in cartoon form. The story has to do with a group of children playing football in the street. The ball smashes a window, a woman looks out of the window, a man makes an ominous gesture, and the children run off. Here is the middle-class version of the story:

> Three boys are playing football and one boy kicks the ball and it goes through the window and the boys are looking at it and a man comes out and shouts at them because they've broken the window so they run away and then that lady looks out of her window and she tells the boys off.

The working-class version is as follows:

They're playing football and he kicks it and it goes through there it breaks the window and they're looking at it and he comes out and shouts at them because they've broken it so they run away and then she looks out and tells them off. (cited in Bernstein 1973c, 203)

Bernstein concludes that the speech of the working-class children is more implicit and context-bound than middle-class speech and that it is less likely that their version would be understood by people who had not seen the picture story.

As Bernstein's ideas developed, the association of class with a particular kind of speech became less rigid. In particular, Bernstein developed the idea of a *code*, one that controls speech according to circumstances. In his later writings on the subject codes are distinguished from *speech variants*. A working-class speaker controlled by a restricted code may on certain occasions, produce an elaborated variant. A middle-class elaborated-code user may on occasions produce a restricted variant. Indeed, in his later writings on the subject, Bernstein relaxed the deterministic aspect of his theory considerably. Not only can restricted-code users produce elaborated variants, but different types of subculture only *tend* to produce certain types of family with certain types of control. These in turn will only *tend* to give rise to speech controlled by a particular code. It has been claimed that by making his theory less deterministic in form, Bernstein fatally compromised its predictive power and hence its scientific usefulness (cf. Stubbs 1976; Toft and Kitwood 1980). Bernstein still stresses that the elaborated code is associated with the development of rationality, the restricted code with authority, metaphor, and the affirmation of personal and social identity (e.g., Bernstein 1971, 190; Bernstein 1973c, 200, where he writes that "restricted codes draw upon metaphor, whereas elaborated codes draw upon rationality"), and that the two codes are "radically different systems of communication" (Bernstein 1971, 166).

One feature of the research of Bernstein and his associates that is held in common with the work of I.Q. theorists is the *quantitative* nature of the data obtained. Put simply, data about language is put into numerical form (scores on tests, length of pauses, number of words or phrases used), and groups of numerical data are compared for social class differences in test score, frequency, or length in order to obtain a picture of what between-class differences (if any) there might be. One question that can be asked of this kind of research is, first of all, how can it give a picture of the use of language in a context of *practical* rationality? and, second, can differences in score, frequency, or length indicate fundamental differences in *constitutive* rationality? (There is, it should be noted, a similar problem for I.Q. theory.)

Not all verbal-deficit theorists rely exclusively on quantitative evidence gathered under fairly formal conditions. In particular, the work of Joan Tough (e.g., Tough 1977a, Tough 1977b) represents an attempt to gain a view of social class differences in language use based on actual speech gathered in a particular context, coupled with a refusal to see it just in an abstract, numerical form. Children from three-and-a-half to seven years of age were recorded talking to their friends in a play situation with a research worker present. The speech of the three-and-a-half–year-olds provides the basis for most of Tough's detailed analysis.

Tough's approach is very similar to that of Bernstein in another way, however, in that it associates rationality-relevant features of language with social class, but without using the concept of code to account for the differences. The children in her study came from markedly different social class backgrounds and were divided into advantaged and disadvantaged groups. Tough's findings are similar to those of Bernstein; she finds, for example, that the advantaged group was better at recognizing causal relationships and in projecting its thinking beyond the immediate situation than the disadvantaged group.

To summarize, the approaches of Tough and Bernstein propose class differences in the exercise of rationality. The language of the lower working class is a less suitable vehicle for rationality than that of the middle class. Bernstein came to elaborate and qualify his theory over the years without abandoning his commitment to formal situations and statistical methods as means of collecting and presenting his material. Tough, on the other hand, preferred to rely on more informal situations and relied more heavily on the transcripts of actual speech in presenting her evidence. Whether either of them fully understood the implications of their research programs is something that will be discussed in the following chapters.

CHAPTER 8

Verbal-deficit theories: the counterattack

I.Q. theory aroused great controversy right from the outset (see Block and Dworkin 1977 for some of the early debates). The same thing happened with verbal-deficit theories. By not focusing on the question of *rationality,* however, many commentators missed the really important part of what Bernstein and others were arguing.

One linguist who did not miss the point but rather took it very much to heart was William Labov. In a famous article, "The Logic of Non-Standard English" (Labov 1969), he faced the Bernstein thesis head on. For many years Labov's paper has been seen by many people as a definitive refutation of verbal-deficit theory. More recently, it has come under attack as being grossly biased, unjust to Bernstein and others, and deeply flawed in its empirical approach (e.g., Honey 1983; Cooper 1984).

Labov accepted that rationality and the ability to reason lay at the core of the controversy about verbal deficit. His first target was the American school of verbal-deficit theorists, notably Bereiter and Engelmann (1966), who decided to treat certain black ghetto children "as if they had no language at all" (Bereiter and Engelmann 1966, 138). Taking their cue from Bernstein, they identify the speech of four–year–old black children from Urbana with the restricted code: "The language of culturally deprived children . . . is not merely an undeveloped version of standard English, but is a basically non–logical mode of expressive behavior" (Bereiter and Engelmann 1966, 113). These remarks go further than Bernstein was prepared to go. He at least was prepared to talk of the logical *simplicity* of the restricted code rather than its *nonlogicality* and indeed, claimed that he never maintained that reasoning was not possible in a restricted code (Bernstein 1973b, 272).

Labov argued that the views of Bereiter and Engelmann and others who thought like them arose from two mistakes. The first mistake was to confuse dialect and style (see Chapter 7) with logicality. For example, the children on Bereiter and Engelmann's program would be taught to answer the question,

"Where is the squirrel?"

not by

"In the tree."

—which, they held, was a nonsentential and hence nonlogical response, but by

"The squirrel is in the tree." (Labov 1969, 184)

Labov's point is that there is a perfectly valid and consistent set of grammatical rules governing nonstandard forms of English such as Black English Vernacular as well as Standard English and that utterances in, for example, Black English Vernacular should not be assessed for grammaticality according to an inappropriate rule system.

The second mistake made by verbal-deficit theorists, according to Labov, was that the situations in which they obtained their speech samples were interviews, which were formal and appeared threatening to the ghetto children involved. The monosyllabic nature of their responses was due, therefore, not to an ability to speak coherently, but to an unwillingness to do so with a large, white (albeit friendly) interviewer.

Do these strictures apply to the work of Bernstein as well as to that of Bereiter and Engelmann? Now, Bernstein does not deny that restricted-code users can reason. He is also at pains to say that he is not concerned with distinctions of dialect and style. It is perfectly possible to maintain that there is a contingent relationship between code and dialect usage; that is, nonstandard dialect and informal-style users just happen to be controlled by a restricted code. In the case of Bernstein, the accusation would gain in substance if the evidence for restricted-code usage was in fact primarily only evidence for the use of a nonstandard dialect or an informal style. This matter will be investigated further in the following chapter. Bernstein's empirical work and that of his associates was carried out in relatively formal settings and did not involve the presentation of speech samples from nonformal settings, so he does seem subject to Labov's strictures on these grounds.

Labov wanted to show that the verbal-deficit hypothesis could not be sustained. He tried to refute it by altering the situations in which the interviews took place—in fact, changing them from interviews into parties and street arguments. The results are by now famous. Best known is the encounter between Larry, a fifteen-year-old gang leader, and John Lewis, a black colleague of Labov. The dialogue between John Lewis and Larry is an important piece of evidence because it involves informal reasoning, and because the main participant is someone whose social background would lead one to expect him to be controlled by a restricted code. I will not quote this exchange immediately, but will instead continue with an account of Labov's views before returning to recent criticisms of them.

Labov hoped that he had brought forward damaging counterevidence against verbal-deficit theory with his informal dialogues with Black English Vernacular speakers. Surprisingly, however, he was not satisfied with this and seemed keen on making a further point, namely, that lower-class speech is a *more* effective tool for reasoning in many ways than is middle-class speech:

> "Is the "elaborated code" of Bernstein really so "flexible, detailed and subtle" as some psychologists believe? . . . Isn't it also turgid, redundant and empty? Is it not simply an elaborated style, rather than a superior code or system? (Labov 1969, 192)

To substantiate this point of view, Labov produced a fairly formal interview between Charles, a college-educated, upper-middle-class black, and Clarence Robins, another colleague of Labov.

> C.R.: Do you know of anything that someone can do, to have someone who has passed on visit them in a dream?
>
> Charles M.: Well, I even heard my parents say that there is such a thing as something in dreams some things like that, and sometimes dream do come true. I have personally never had a dream come true. I've never dreamt that someone was dying and they actually died, (Mhm) or that I was going to have ten dollars the next day and somehow I got ten dollars in my pocket (Mhm). I don't particularly believe in that, I don't think it's true. I do feel though that there is such a thing as—ah—witchcraft. I do feel that in certain cultures there is such a thing as witchcraft, or some sort of *science* of witchcraft; I don't think it's just a matter of believing hard enough that there is such a thing as witchcraft. I do believe that there is such a thing that a person can put himself in a state of *mind* (Mhm), or that—er—something could be given them to intoxicate them in a certain—to a certain frame of mind—that—that could actually be considered witchcraft. (Labov 1969, 197–98)

According to Labov, Charles's argument displays a high degree of verbosity and he actually says very little while employing a lot of words:

> Without the extra verbiage and the O.K. words like *science, culture* and *intoxicate*, Charles M. appears as something less than a first rate thinker. The initial impression of him as a good speaker is simply our long-conditioned reaction to middle class verbosity: we know that people who use these stylistic devices are educated people and we are inclined to credit them with saying something intelligent. (Labov 1969, 199–200)

This interpretation of Charles has been hotly disputed recently by Honey (1983) and Cooper (1984). Cooper, while not wishing to defend

Bernstein's position particularly, takes issue with Labov's treatment of Charles. Briefly, he makes the following points: Charles's speech is a monologue, Larry's interview (see below) is heavily prompted. Labov employs literary devices to encourage a negative attitude to Charles, like putting his hesitations in brackets, describing Charles as a "good" speaker in scare quotes and characterizing Charles's language as the "proper" medium for formal writing and public communication (Labov 1969, 197–98), also in scare quotes. Finally, he goes out of his way to provide an unsympathetic interpretation of Charles's monologue. Cooper points out that some small knowledge of anthropology, for example, of the work of Evans-Pritchard, would lead one to realize that what Charles is saying may stem from an informed interest in the subject. Charles's argument is not subjected to helpful reconstruction. For example, Labov's interpretation of Charles's argument goes as follows.

(1) Some people say that dreams come true.
(2) I have never had a dream come true.
(3) Therefore I don't believe (1).

Cooper points out that in his conclusion Charles denies that he believes that dreams come true, not proposition (1). But furthermore, a sympathetic interpreter could easily have rendered the argument more compelling by inserting a concealed premise (to make the argument an enthymeme) to which Charles would find no difficulty in assenting, into the argument—namely, that, in the area of the supernatural, personal experience rather than hearsay is the only rational ground for belief (Cooper 1984, 182).

Cooper is at pains to point out that he does not know if this interpretation of Charles's monologue is the correct one, but simply insists that there are no interpretative subleties about construing it this way (Labov 1969, 185). One could go further and say that in seeking to understand a talk, conversation, or any verbal exchange one should, the absence of any convincing evidence to the contrary, assume the reasonableness of the speakers. This principle is very similar to that proclaimed by Grandy (1973) and known as the Principle of Humanity, that in seeking to understand and interpret people of a culture very different from our own, we should seek, wherever possible, to make their thought and actions seem reasonable and rational unless there is good evidence for the contrary assumption.

Note that the assumption is not merely that the speakers are constitutively rational, but that they are *reasonable,* that is, they advance good arguments for their beliefs and act in ways consistent with what they are trying to do in the context in which they are trying to do it. In other words, it is assumed that they are at least fairly capable theoretical and practical reasoners. This assumption might have to be abandoned if evidence to the contrary appeared, but in the absence of such evidence, it is a sound methodological principle. If we adopt this practice for Charles, and Cooper is surely right to suggest that we do, then it should be adopted for Larry the gang leader as well. It is clear enough that Labov wants to do this in the case of Larry, but against his intentions, he does not succeed very well. To see why this is so, it is necessary to look at the exchange between Larry and John Lewis.

Labov is at pains to create a situation where Larry is on familiar ground. His interlocutor is black and a Black English Vernacular speaker, and Larry is invited to take part in a verbal battle of wits with no serious consequences, a situation with which he must have been familiar in his life on the street corners.

J.L.:   What happens to you after you die? Do you know?

Larry: Yeah, I know.

J.L.:   What?

Larry: After they put you in the ground, your body turns into—ah—bones an' shit.

J.L.:   What happens to your spirit?

Larry: Your spirit—soon as you die, your spirit leaves you.

J.L.:   And where does the spirit go?

Larry: Well, it all depends . . .

J.L.:   On what?

Larry: You know, like some people say if you're good an' shit, your spirit goin' t'heaven . . . 'n if you bad, your spirit goin' to hell. Well, bullshit! Your spirit goin' to hell anyway, good or bad.

J.L.:   Why?

Larry: Why? I'll tell you why. 'Cause, you see, doesn' nobody really know that it's a God, y'know, 'cause I mean, I have seen black gods, pink gods, white gods, all colour gods, and don't nobody know its really a God. An' when they be sayin' if you good you goin' t' heaven, tha's bullshit, 'cause you ain't goin' to no heaven, 'cause it ain't no heaven for you to go to.

J.L.:   Well, if there's no heaven, how could there be a hell?

Larry: I mean—ye—eah. Well, let me tell you, it ain't no hell, 'cause this is hell right here, y'know!

J.L.: This is hell?

Larry: Yeah, this is hell right here!

J.L.: . . . But just say there is a God, what colour is he? White or black?

Larry: Well, if it is a God . . . I wouldn't know what colour he really *would* be.

J.L.: But now, jus' suppose there was a God—

Larry: Unless'n they say . . .

J.L.: No, I was jus' sayin' jus' suppose there is a God, would he be white or black?

Larry: He'd be white man.

J.L.: Why?

Larry: Why? I'll tell you why. 'Cause the average whitey out here got everything, you dig? And the nigger ain't got shit, y'know? Y'understan'? So—um—in order for *that* to happen, you know it ain't no black God that's doin' that bullshit. (Labov 1969, 193–96).

Labov comments on this passage:

> No one can hear Larry's answer to this question without being convinced that they are in the presence of a skilled speaker with great "verbal presence of mind," who can use the English language expertly for many purposes. (Labov 1969, 196–97).

Cooper does not doubt this statement, but tries to show that the virtues of Larry's performance are those of rhetoric and sophistry, rather than genuine concern for consistency and reasonableness. For example, Larry moves from

(1) Nobody knows that there is a God.

to

(2) There is no God.

—which is the proposition that is needed for Larry to draw the conclusion that there is no heaven. In other words, Larry is quite willing to bend the rules of logic in order to win the argument. Cooper argues that Labov is employing double standards in trying to put Larry's behavior in a favorable light in comparison with Charles's.

It is quite clear that Cooper is onto something in his criticisms of

Labov. What appears to have happened is that Labov failed to distinguish between two objectives in his article, one of which was a reasonable one, namely the claim that Standard English and Black English Vernacular are both vehicles of rationality and that each is as adequate as the other in this respect, and the claim that Black English Vernacular is better in this respect than Standard English, which is a less plausible claim.

Labov does seem to have provided biased interpretations of Larry and Charles, ones that work in the former's favor. Cooper's observation is quite decisive as an objection to the claim that the dialogues are evidence for the superior rationality of Black English Vernacular. Against the claim that Standard English is superior to Black English Vernacular, one would have to show that Larry was not a rational or a reasonable speaker and that Charles was. Cooper claims that this is no part of his purpose, but his own treatment of Larry suggests that he is less than sympathetic to his abilities as a thinker, and indeed willing to show his unreasonableness.

It is true that Larry does try to "bend the rules of logic," but in the context of what he is doing, namely, trying to win an argument, this is quite reasonable (as a practical objective). This does not mean to say that anything goes, because when Larry is picked up on a point—for example, when he is asked if there is no heaven, how could there be a hell?—he is forced to give his position some consistency. So although his practical objective is to win an argument (at a not very high level of seriousness), it is incumbent on the other participant to point out a fallacy or an inconsistency if there is one. There is nothing unusual about this: in all forms of debate, whether serious or not, it is up to the opponent, if he is to press his case, to detect and to point out fallacies.

The *practical* objective might be to win a client's case, obtain a job, or win a motion of no confidence. Although rhetorical tricks are a legitimate move, they can be overridden by an appeal to the rules of theoretical reason. A bad argument, once detected, must either be abandoned or modified until it becomes more acceptable.

Cooper detects further evidence of Larry's illogicality. He does so by relying on Labov's own interpretation of a passage of Larry's argument. Curiously, he does so while commenting on Labov's "ignorance of logic." Labov comments that Larry's basic argument is to deny the twin propositions

(A) If you are good   (B) Then your spirit will go to heaven

($-$A) If you are bad   (C) Then your spirit will go to hell

Larry denies B and asserts that if (A) or ($-$A) then C. (i.e., if you are good or bad, your spirit will go to hell anyway).

What Labov appears to be suggesting is that Larry is denying *both* if you are good then your spirit will go to heaven *and* if you are bad then your spirit will go to hell. As Cooper points out, if he is denying both these conditional propositions, then he is implicitly contradicting himself because he cannot have it that both (1) It is not true that if you are bad then your spirit is going to hell, and (2) Good or bad, your spirit is going to hell anyway.

This is right, but is it what Larry is saying? Labov, especially if he is ignorant of logic, will be a poor guide here. What Larry actually *says* is

> You know, like some people say if you're good an' shit, your spirit goin' t' heaven . . . 'n if you bad, your spirit goin' to hell. Well bullshit!

An interpretation of Larry as a reasonable speaker would take him to be denying the joint proposition:

> "If you are good then your spirit is going to heaven and if you are bad then your spirit is goin' to hell."

In logical notation this can be expressed:

$$-([if\ A\ then\ B])\ and\ [if\ -A\ then\ C]).$$

To treat Labov's interpretation as the right one would indeed make Larry appear unreasonable because, on this account, having denied that if you are bad then your spirit is going to hell, he affirms that good or bad your spirit is going to hell, and he does this almost immediately. What is more, what Larry is denying follows as a conclusion from

> An' when they be sayin' if you good, you goin' t'heaven tha's bullshit.

$$i.e.,\ -\ (if\ A\ then\ B).$$

Furthermore, if we allow Larry the hidden premise

> "Your spirit is going to hell,"

$$i.e.,\ C$$

then it will serve as a premise for the argument that concludes that:

$$if\ (A\ or\ -A)\ then\ C,$$

i.e., Your spirit is goin' to hell anyway, good or bad (see appendix to this chapter).

Larry could reasonably be allowed C by a sympathetic interpreter, as he holds that (1) when you die your spirit leaves you, (2) there is no heaven for you to go to, and (3) this is hell right here. Your spirit would then go to hell because there is nowhere else for it to go.

One important point that Cooper makes must be noted at once. Larry begins by asserting his conclusion, i.e.,

> You know, like some people say if you're good an' shit, you're spirit goin' t'heaven . . . 'n if you bad, your spirit goin' to hell. Well, bullshit! Your spirit goin' to hell anyway, good or bad.

Most of the premises and intermediate steps that go to support this conclusion are inserted *subsequently* after questioning by John Lewis. Now, although much everyday reason and argument takes this form, it is not directly comparable with Charles's argument, and a sympathetic (although by no means exaggerated) interpretation is needed to present Larry as a speaker of the same logical acumen as Labov suggests he is.

What is the significance of Labov's article in the verbal-deficit controversy? Cooper claims that there is little value either in the comparison between Larry and Charles or in Labov's presentation of Larry as an acute verbal reasoner. Consequently, Labov's article, despite its being widely cited as damaging counterevidence to the claims of verbal-deficit theorists, is in fact, of little value in this matter.

I do not share this view. Nevertheless, a fuller assessment of Labov's work must wait until the next chapter. Two points should be noted, for they are important to an understanding of the research that followed Bernstein's original work. First of all, unlike Bernstein, Labov used an informal speech setting with which the subject was reasonably familiar. Second, the evidence presented was of *what was actually said* in an interpretative context, so that it is possible to make sense of what is going on given the speaker's motivation and cultural background.

This "naturalistic turn" in sociolinguistic research led to a change of emphasis that not only moved beyond merely counting the occurrence of items of grammar, vocabulary, pausing, etc., but also took into consideration the actual context of what was said. This proved to be the case even for such scholars as Joan Tough who tried to develop verbal-deficit theory in a way different from that of Bernstein and his associates. Most noteworthy in this respect is the longitudinal study undertaken by Gordon Wells and his associates (Wells 1975, Wells 1977, Wells 1987, for example), in which the talk of children with their parents was monitored on a random basis throughout the day by means of microphones attached to the subjects, which were activated at irregular times during the day. The object of this was to minimize what Labov (1972) called the "Observer's Paradox," whereby the subject's awareness of the fact that he or she is being monitored has itself a significant effect on talk.

The findings of Wells et al. do not confirm the verbal-deficit hypothesis. There are differences in the way in which mothers talk to their children and try to develop their linguistic skills, but there is no strong connection with social class. Wells (1977), in particular, makes this point in relation to Tough (1977a) and argues, among other things, that she does not look at speech in the context of what the speakers are trying to say to each other, but relates speech only to a "graded taxonomy of decontextualised functions" (Wells 1977, 20). In other words, in naturalistic research it is not enough merely to present what people have actually said, one needs to place it in the context of the practice and circumstances that alone allow the listener to make sense of it. Wells also argues that Tough fails to provide an adequate continuum of social class comparisons, comparing only advantaged with disadvantaged social groups. Wells (1981) reports significant class differences in the introduction of children to literary materials and techniques, differences reflected in subsequent school performance. The significance of this and other findings will be further discussed in Chapters 11 and 12.

Another, smaller-scale, naturalistic study by Tizard and Hughes (1984) reports little difference in the verbal upbringing of children from different social classes. All children are listened and talked to, and all develop much the same degree of verbal ability. The authors do report certain differences in emphasis between parents from different social classes in such matters as introducing their children to a wide range of general knowledge and vocabulary, and encouraging them to be more explicit in answering questions:

> These differences seemed to us to amount to a difference in language style and educational approach, rather than to a "language deficit" in working class homes. All the basic language usages were observed in the homes: the social class difference was in the frequency of the usages. Further, the differences we have described refer to group averages. Within each social class group, there was a wide range of language usage. (Tizard and Hughes 1984, 252–53).

Before concluding this chapter, certain other criticisms of a more theoretical nature of the work of Bernstein and Tough ought to be mentioned. Stubbs (1976), Jackson (1974), and Toft and Kitwood (1980) all refer to the increasing vagueness and difficulty of verifying or refuting the theory of restricted and elaborated codes. Rosen (1974) draws attention to Bernstein's inadequate conception of social class and Dittmar (1976) to an alleged incoherence in the formulation of the codes theory. It is well beyond the scope of this book to consider all these matters. What I have hoped to establish in this and the previous chapter is that verbal-deficit theory is about the adequacy of language for the expression of rationality. For any version of verbal-deficit theory to be accepted, it will need (1) to formulate what sense or senses of rationality are supposed to differ between different groups, and (2) to establish that evidence for those differences is, in the first place, appropriate and, in the second place, adequate. These matters will concern us in Chapter 9.

Appendix to chapter 8

Formal proofs of two of Larry's arguments.

a) To prove − [if A then B) & (if−A then C] from − (if A then B).

   (1) −(if A then B)   Larry's assertion.
   (2) (if A then B) & (if −A then C)   Assumption.
   (3) If A then B   & elimination, (2).
   (4) (if A then B) & −(if A then B)   & introduction, (1), (3)
   (5) −[(if A then B) & [if −A then C)]   Reduction ad absurdum (4),
                                                discharging (2).

b) To prove If (A or −A) then C, from C.

   (1) A or −A   Assumption.
   (2) C   Assumption.
   (3) (A or −A) & C   From (1) and (2) by
                                                   & introduction.
   (4) C   From (3) by & elimination.
   (5) If (A or −A) then C   From (3), (4) by conditional
                                                   proof, discharging (1).

I am grateful to Professor David Cooper for suggestions regarding the first of these proofs.

CHAPTER 9

Verbal-deficit theories: an overview

It is no part of my purpose in this chapter to sift through the vast amounts of evidence for and against the truth of verbal-deficit theories. What I hope to do is to put forward and defend an attitude to these theories that, if accepted, will allow the reader to assess the merits or flaws of that evidence. In the first place, we need to remind ourselves that Bereiter, Engelmann, Bernstein, Tough, and others took their stand on the alleged inferior capacity for reason and rationality of lower-class language. What does this claim amount to?

It was argued in Chapter 2 that there was a sense of "rationality" that referred to the structural capacity of a language for expressing reason and thought. It is possible to imagine a language without the structure that makes reasoning possible, made up of simple signs that only have significance when used on their own. This seems to be what Bereiter and Engelmann thought ghetto language was like. At a higher level we could imagine the Bernsteinian concept of a logically simple language with a limited set of logical operators. Such a language could, for example, contain negation and conjunction but not be capable of expressing tense and generality. Indeed, Bernstein's frequent insistence on the *implicitness* or the *context dependence* of the restricted code suggests that he does, at times, have something like this in mind. Another approach to this question of classification is to adopt the approach of Tough and give a taxonomy of rationality-relevant functions that speech may be said to fulfill or fail to fulfill.

In these cases one is talking of differences in constitutive rationality between the "lower" and the "higher" varieties (cf. Gordon 1981 for this form of classification of verbal-deficit theories). A contrast is made between middle-class speech, which contains all the logical functions, and lower-class speech, which contains either none or—at best—a subset. This is the most ambitious form of verbal-deficit theory and also the most Platonic in form, going further than I.Q. theory (in most of its versions) in assigning a definite *qualititative* rather than *quantitative* difference to the thought that can be expressed by the high and low varieties.

There is, however, another approach to classification, one that verbal-deficit theorists, notably Bernstein, often slide into, possibly without being fully aware of the significance of the shift. This approach assumes the structural similarity of high and low varieties but asserts that, as a matter of fact, speakers of high varieties (associated with the middle class) use their linguistic resources more ably than speakers of low varieties (associated particularly with the lower working class). For example, Bernstein writes about the lack of logical sequence in restricted code speech: "The thoughts are often strung together like beads on a frame rather than following a planned sequence" (Bernstein 1965, 158).

But the differences extend not merely to theoretical reason but to practical reason as well. Lower-class speakers cannot relate the present to the future, have low levels of curiosity and a poor conception of causality, and have difficulty in carrying out long-term projects. This may be due to different levels of constitutive rationality, but it may also be due to a difference in the level of skill that is employed by lower-working-class and other speakers in exploiting the common linguistic resources that they both have available to them.

Finally, the differences may be ones of *contextual* rationality—that is, lower-class speakers may have different levels of skill in responding to the demands of the situation in particular contexts. For example, the high-variety speaker may be better able to cope with formal linguistic situations such as discussions or interviews, he or she may have superior access to specialized vocabularies or be better able to cope with the demands of reading and writing. It should be said, however, that if this last version is what the verbal-deficit theorist is claiming, then it becomes misleading to describe his or her position as one that ascribes *cognitive* differences to the two modes of speech. There are merely, in this version, differences of style, dialect, and technique between the two varieties. The thesis loses its Platonic character and becomes more akin to the Rousseauist view that opportunity is unequally distributed, or to the cultural-interest view that particular abilities, including specialized linguistic abilities, are better developed in some subcultures than in others (see Chapter 3).

What kind of evidence could be brought forward to sustain these different versions of the verbal-deficit thesis? Let us take the view first of all that differences between high and low varieties are differences in levels of constitutive rationality. In this case, some logical constructions will be available in variety A that will not be available in variety B. Reasonable samples from both variety A and variety B speakers would show that certain constructions, for example "all" or "some" were used and understood by A speakers but were not used and understood by B speakers.

To refute this thesis it would only be necessary to show that speakers characterized as B speakers by some independent criterion, say social class or family structure, were in fact capable of using and understanding such constructions. Cooper makes a similar point even more forcefully in relation to dialect and logical capacity when he writes that the equation between dialect and logical capacity is dissolved when a single speaker of, say, Black English Vernacular is found whose capacity for logical analysis is not deficient "however atypical he/she may be in various respects" (Cooper 1984, 179).

On this criterion, the evidence of Bernstein, Tough, and others simply will not do. For what they present are differences in the *frequency of usage* of certain items, in other words, speakers of variety A (the elaborated code) use certain items more frequently than do speakers of variety B (the restricted code). That is, both groups use the items, contrary to the hypothesis (a point made by Stubbs 1976). Worse than this, the items that are used with differing frequencies are not even obviously *rationality-relevant*, that is, they are not items of logical structure like for example "possibly," "necessarily," or the examples given earlier, which would be expressive of constitutive rationality, and which would permit a certain range of logical argument and reasoning. For example, there are differences in the frequency with which subordinate clauses, the passive voice ("he was hit by me," rather than the active "I hit him"), uncommon adjectives, adverbs, conjunctions, and egocentric sequences (like "I mean" and "I think") are used by middle-class speakers compared with working class speakers, middle-class speakers using these items more frequently (cf. Bernstein 1962b, 135).

Such evidence is at a great distance from showing the "logical simplicity" of working-class language. As most verbal-deficit theory evidence either for or against is of this sort, it may safely be dismissed as insufficient evidence for any differences in constitutive rationality, whatever other significance it may have. An exception to this is the evidence presented in Bernstein (1960) to the effect that public (i.e., independent) schoolboys scored better on the Mill Hill vocabulary test compared with Post Office messengers. For them to have done this, they would have had to score absolutely better on some items than the messengers. Scrutiny of the Mill Hill test does not help the case, however, because this test assesses recognition of items of vocabulary and, at its highest levels, latinate vocabulary that might be used in formal styles; it does not test logical items at all. As Bernstein was at pains to make it clear that he was not concerned with items of style and dialect, far from being corroborative evidence these findings are, if anything, somewhat embarrassing to the codes hypothesis.

If the strong, constitutive-rationality version of verbal-deficit theory does not hold, then does the normative version, which asserts that there are differences in practical and/or theoretical rationality expressed in high and low versions of a structurally identical language? Will frequency differences show this? If variety A speakers use more logical items than variety B speakers, will this show that they are better reasoners? (cf. Inhelder and Piaget 1958).

Unfortunately, the evidence presented by verbal-deficit theorists is not of differences in the frequency of usage of *logical* items, so it is difficult to see how this reinterpretation of the theory would help. Would a count of the use of logical items help to establish differences in the ability to reason? If A speakers used the "if . . . then . . . " construction more frequently than B speakers, would this show that A speakers were more adept in the use of the conditional than B speakers? It is hard to see why it should. Just because I drive a car more frequently than you does not of itself make me a better driver. But let us consider a particular case. Here are two arguments, one valid, the other invalid:

(1)   If Wrexham is in North Wales then Wrexham is in Europe
      Wrexham is in Europe.
      Therefore, Wrexham is in North Wales.
(2)   If Pittsburgh is a steel-making city then Pittsburgh is an industrial city.
      Pittsburgh is a steel-making city.
      Therefore, Pittsburgh is an industrial city.

(1) is invalid, (2) is valid; both use "if . . . then . . . " once each. But this fact *of itself* tells us nothing about the reasoning abilities of those who employed the arguments. What matters is whether or not the arguments are valid or invalid, or, more generally, good or bad. Here, frequency of the usage of a logical item is of no help.

Perhaps the case of verbal-deficit theory would be helped by comparing the *frequency* with which A and B speakers use valid or invalid arguments. If A speakers use them more frequently than B speakers, then this could be taken as evidence favorable to verbal-deficit theory. Tempting though this suggestion is, there are serious pitfalls to it. We have already seen in the previous chapter the difficulty of establishing just *which* arguments are being used by a particular speaker on a particular occasion. In informal situations (but also in relatively formal situations, such as Charles's interview), a sympathetic interpretation of the speaker is necessary if we are to make sense of what Charles says. A variety of interpretations of a passage of argument may be possible, even when the interpreter is sympathetic.

However, another difficulty presents itself even when we have the speech, the sympathetic interpreter, and an accepted argument form at hand. The difficulty is this. The use of language generally and reason and argument in particular take place in the context of what a speaker is trying to do and the social and cultural context in which he or she is trying to do it. This is particularly clear in the case of the exchange between Larry and John Lewis. The cultural context in which the exchange takes place is a street argument where a boy's standing in the group is enhanced by his ability to win arguments. Therefore his practical objective is to "win" the exchange, that is, to appear to have the better of the encounter. Although this is not precisely the situation in Larry's encounter with John Lewis—there does not, for example, appear to be an audience of other youths—it is sufficiently similar to make it recognizably that kind of exchange.

Larry uses the rules of logic when it suits him and also bends them when it suits him. He is only constrained when an objection or an infraction is pointed out, and this is solely due to the quickwittedness of his codisputant. In other words, theoretical reason is subordinated to the practical objective of winning the argument, as far as appearances go at least. This is a fairly typical situation, the use of rhetorical devices is not confined to the street corner, but can be found as well in the classroom, courtroom, and debating chamber.

"Perhaps," a verbal-deficit theorist might argue, "we can overcome these difficulties by isolating the practical effects, studying speakers in a neutral situation rather like experimental conditions in the natural sciences, where extraneous factors like cultural conditioning and personal motivation do not apply." This argument would, if convincing, be a neat justification for the use of formal interview and survey techniques to gain information about language use. Unfortunately, the analogy with experimental science does not hold in sociolinguistics. There are two reasons for this. The first is that interviews are an established sort of encounter, usually a formal and often a stressful sort, where verbal exchanges are often colored by wariness, disingenuity, cunning, and anxiety. One only has to consider such situations as job hunting, police inquiries, or a television appearance to appreciate this point.

A formal interview of this sort is bound to affect the perception and motivation of the subject. Labov drew attention to the wariness and anxiety of many subjects under these conditions. An educated person, more familiar with social-science research, may see more clearly and be more cooperative with the requirement to make a verbal display under these conditions (a point made by Edwards 1980).

A second consideration is that there can be no isolation of extraneous factors in the required sense, because people are bound to relate their perceptions of the present situation to their larger concerns and to the culture they live in. They may respond by giving a verbal display to impress the interviewer, by being neutral about the proceedings, or even by being hostile or sullen. This point applies to survey data as well, where people are asked about what they would have said in such and such a situation (e.g., Robinson and Rackstraw 1972). It may be extremely difficult to do this; one may reply saying what one feels one *ought* to have said in the situation, especially if one has, as a middle-class educated person, some notion of what might be the "right" reply as far as the interviewer is concerned.

A way around this difficulty might be the introduction of informal interview techniques. Here the subject is asked questions in a "natural" setting. The difficulty now is that whereas formal interviews have an established social role, it is far from clear just what is the role of an informal interview:

> The formal interview is a recognized speech event in our society. Members of the speech community know the rules of speaking for interviews. They expect to be asked a series of questions and to answer them. Although being interviewed is hardly an everyday experience for most people, there is nothing "artificial" or "unnatural" about it, and there is no reason to believe that the speech produced by the subject in such an interaction is anything but natural— for an interview (Wolfson 1976, 195).

As Wolfson puts it so well, it is extremely difficult to see the point of an informal interview, for adults or for children, unless it is perceived that some kind of verbal display is called for. Much "language development" that goes on in nurseries and infant schools is of this informal interview variety, and, as Tizard and Hughes (1984) point out, such situations often have little communicative value, for it is not clear to the subject just what is wanted by the interviewer.

Labov's own data might seem open to this objection, but his achievement seems to have been in recognizing this danger and then using recognizable linguistic encounters such as a party or a street argument, whose rules and context were understood by both researcher and subject. Before I return to the significance of the work of Labov and other researchers, it is worth looking briefly at the empirical results of Bernstein and his associates in order to see how they fit into the pattern of language use in the context of practical rationality. Bernstein (1962a) and Hawkins (1973) report differences in the rate of pausing between working-class and middle-class speakers. Pausing is taken to indicate planning. Middle-class speakers were found to pause more than working-class speakers, and this was taken to indicate better-planned speech on their part.

On the approach recommended in this chapter, the criterion for how well-planned the speech is will be just what is said in the particular context, personal and social, in which it is said. The only direct way of determining whether or not someone is speaking thoughtfully is by looking at what he or she says in context. Pausing by itself tells us very little; it may, for example, be due to uncertainty rather than to planning, as Hawkins himself acknowledges. Hawkins's own technique for overcoming the problem, distinguishing between different kinds of pauses (cf. Hawkins 1973), is not very convincing, and his own results are not all that decisive.

Another paper by Hawkins (1969) is often cited as crucial support for verbal-deficit theory. We have already looked at this experiment in Chapter 7. Two groups of children were asked to recount a picture story in their own words. The different approaches to the task were seen as evidence of the *context dependence* of working-class children's speech. Clearly, this could be a finding of great importance. We saw in Chapter 2 how the ability to use language to talk and think about matters beyond the immediate spatiotemporal context is a very important ability of the elaborated-code speaker. If Hawkins had really offered evidence that the lower working class lacked such an ability, this would obviously be good evidence for a "strong" version of verbal-deficit theory.

However, Hawkins showed much less than that. In the first place, as has been noted by numerous commentators, a context-dependent approach to the task was the one suggested by practical rationality, as the picture sequence was present to both the children and the interviewer. Second, Edwards (1976) has produced evidence to suggest that when the need to produce more context-independent speech was perceived and understood by working-class children, they were perfectly able to do so in a task-oriented situation. Third, Hawkins (1977) has admitted that the famous transcripts were 'slightly exaggerated' versions of *many* transcripts of middle and working-class children, not actual transcripts of what *particular* children said. Bernstein has admitted that Hawkins's results do not demonstrate that working-class children cannot, in certain contexts, produce context-independent speech (Bernstein 1972, 221). What, then, is the significance of Labov's evidence? We have seen that in one respect it is flawed, especially in the matter of the unfair treatment of Charles. But if we reject the view that lower-class language is a *superior* medium for reasoning in comparison with middle-class language, does the Larry interview show that verbal-deficit theory is in some way flawed? Let us consider some of the objections to Labov. Larry's exchange is an isolated and untypical example of lower-class speech. This is an objection against the view that lower-class language is a *better* medium for rationality than middle-class language, as Cooper (1984) points out, where it becomes crucial that Larry and Charles are typical and representative speakers from their communities. However Larry, if he is accepted, does refute the view that lower-class language as such is a poor medium for reasoning.

Second, it is objected that Labov's work concerns the capacity of a *dialect* for logical reasoning rather than a *code* and is hence not really relevant to the claims of verbal-deficit theory. Halliday has suggested, for example, that Larry is speaking in a way that suggests that he is controlled predominantly by an elaborated code (Halliday 1978, 86–87), while Lee comments that:

> Although Labov, for example, uses his argument about the logic of non-standard forms to refute Bernstein's theory of codes, the issue is of a different order and comments about different dialects cannot refute or support evidence concerning elaborated or restricted codes. So although a working class/urban black child's speech is correct and logical according to the dialect he uses,

he *may* still be operating in a restricted code, whereas an elaborated code may help to determine success in schools as they are. (Lee 1981, 103)

Lee is being equivocal about the meaning of "logical" in the phrase "correct and logical." "Logical" in this sense means "consistent according to the grammar of the dialect." What is, of course, at issue is whether or not Larry's speech is logical as a piece of reasoning. Everyone speaks in some dialect, and lower-class dialect may as a matter of fact be associated with a "low" variety of speaking in the verbal-deficit sense. The question is, Is Larry's speech of a "low" variety?

Halliday is right if all he means is "if one reasons, then one's speech is controlled by an elaborated code," and "Larry is reasoning, therefore he is using an elaborated code." But there are two difficulties with this line, if it is accepted. First of all, there is an independent causal condition for the emergence of restricted codes. The deprived social background of people like Larry is said to give rise to operation with a restricted code. Why then is it not doing so in the case of Larry? The second difficulty is that Larry's speech is full of the markers of a restricted code, namely, the use of egocentric sequences ("I know . . . "), sympathetic circularity ("Well let me tell you . . . ," "You dig?" "Why, I'll tell you why . . . "), etc., as well as markers of an elaborated code, marking tentativeness or distance from an opinion, for example: "I wouldn't know . . . ," "I couldn't say . . . ," "I mean. . . ." It would appear that the linguistic-code criteria do not work well as measures of reasoning, and that the sociological criteria for the emergence of code usage do not predict well either. On the face of it, this must be a damaging counterexample to the verbal-deficit thesis. Not only is Larry *constitutively* rational in the same way as a middle-class speaker, he also seems to be adept as a practical and theoretical reasoner, if we adopt a sympathetic interpretation, in much the same way as we can do for Charles.

A recent, highly influential study of Bernstein's work (Atkinson 1985) suggests that the act of explicating and interpreting the Larry dialogue is an exercise of doubtful legitimacy, somehow transforming Larry's thoughts into something more than they are (Atkinson 1985, 106–7). There is, however, nothing wrong with providing a sympathetic *interpretation* of what a speaker is saying, if the speaker is not available to do so himself. Neither Cooper nor I claim that we have definitively captured what Larry and Charles *meant* but only that they can plausibly be represented as having meant what the interpretations suggest they mean (Labov is more definite about the meaning of the extracts than is really warranted by the evidence). Cooper's sympathetic interpretation of Charles and my sympathetic interpretation of Larry do not distort but rather clarify what they meant if we assume them to be talking sense of some kind. Neither Labov nor I has turned Larry into a "sophisticated logician" as Atkinson claims; we have tried, rather, to show how he operates as a skilled debater. Strangely,

Atkinson does not object to Cooper's article, which provides the same *kind* of treatment of Labov's subjects as Labov himself, although with somewhat different conclusions.

Of course, Labov's example is an isolated one. But if the methodology is sound, other evidence that relies on natural settings and actual examples of speech should corroborate much of what Labov has argued. I have tried to show that formal settings and quantitative data *alone* are not appropriate means for testing the verbal-deficit hypothesis. On the other hand, the use of quantitative data, where appropriate, together with naturalistic settings and speech, should give us a clearer view of the state of verbal-deficit theory at the present time.

The work of Wells and his associates (already cited), which was a long-term naturalistic study, does not corroborate the verbal-deficit hypothesis, and neither do the smaller-scale naturalistic studies of Wootton (1974) and Tizard and Hughes (1984). It is fair to conclude, then, that verbal-deficit theories in either their constitutive or normative versions are not very convincing as a guide to understanding class or group difference in educational achievement. I do not wish the reader to conclude that the verbal-deficit controversy is a whole lot of fuss about nothing. There are important issues at stake for education, but it is a matter of teasing them out and of refraining from bold generalizations and over-bold hypotheses. I will, in particular, consider the view that there are differences in the way in which social groups approach certain linguistic situations that may equip them unequally for tasks pertinent to educational achievement. In other words, I will consider the language of different classes with respect to their suitability for certain *contextual* forms of rationality. In Chapter 10 the spoken word will be looked at and, in Chapter 11, the written word.

Before finishing this survey of verbal-deficit theory, it is worth looking at the views of John Honey (1983), which have made a certain impact in this area of controversy. Like Cooper, he criticizes Labov, for a biased and unscientific approach. Unlike Cooper, he is prepared to challenge the view put forward here that all known languages share roughly the same level of structural complexity or as he puts it, the view that "all languages are equally good" (Honey 1983, 5). Honey adopts the view of Edward Sapir and Benjamin Lee Whorf that language influences thought (known as the Sapir–Whorf hypothesis, cf. Sapir 1921, Whorf 1955). In itself this is an innocuous idea, but when it is coupled with the view that words stand for meanings in the mind (e.g. Sapir 1921, 11–12) and the view that there is a fairly neat correspondence between grammatical and logical distinctions (e.g., Honey 1983, 11), it is easy to fall into the temptation of thinking that different cultures (or even individuals) inhabit their own "thought worlds" of distinct meaning and logical structure. From this conception it is not difficult to postulate forms of language that are *less adequate* than others for certain purposes.

Bernstein acknowledges a large debt to Sapir and Whorf in his formulation of the codes theory (Bernstein 1973a, 23).

This is not the place to consider the vast topic of the nature of meaning, but some comments on the distinction between grammatical and logical aspects of language are appropriate. Honey makes three criticisms of the view that "all languages are equally good." His first point is that some languages have richer fields of vocabulary than others and can thus describe ranges of experience and nuances of meaning that other languages, lacking such a field of vocabulary, cannot. His second point is that *literacy* opens up types of thinking and experience ("objective knowledge" and "critical thinking") that are not available to preliterate societies. This view will be dealt with fully in Chapter 11. His third argument is that grammatical constructions permit some thought patterns that languages that do not contain such constructions cannot allow.

Honey is operating under two confusions in arguing like this. One preliminary point to make, however, is that any attack on the notion that "all languages are equally good," should also explain what that phrase means. Honey's first confusion is to run together the idea of the *social adequacy* of a language for a certain purpose, let us say for getting on in a career, with its *logical adequacy* for certain purposes, for example, for formulating hypotheses or expressing the ideas of possibility and necessity. As this confusion is particularly related to verbal-deficit theories and educational achievement, it will be looked at more closely in Chapter 10. The second confusion is directly related to the matter under discussion and will be dealt with at once. Honey has failed to look at different levels of language. In particular, he has failed to distinguish between constitutive and contextual aspects of the concept of rationality (see Chapter 2).

Some cultures have clearly developed certain ranges of activity much more than others. Western society in particular has developed science and technology to a far greater degree than any other culture in the world. This has involved the development of attitudes of mind, techniques such as mathematics and the experimental method, characteristic ways of reasoning, and vocabularies distinctive to this sort of practice. These ways of reasoning are not, however, *fundamentally* distinct from other ways of reasoning in any other society. Like any other participants in an activity that has its characteristic aims and methods, the scientist builds on an enormous background of tacitly understood common knowledge and assumptions. When he reasons, he does so against a background of that knowledge and those assumptions, employing them as suppressed premises (enthymemes) and intermediate steps in his arguments.

It is, of course, true that the vocabulary of one culture cannot simply be inserted into the vocabulary of another and thereby become intelligible to that culture. Hunter–gatherers, for example, could not talk intelligbly about quantum physics if some appropriate vocabulary were to be inserted into their language. They lack a whole outlook, form of experience and conceptual structure in which the concepts of quantum physics would be intelligible. This is not to say that a tribe of aborigines, for example, inhabits a different thought world or even a different reality from that of those who are part of Western civilization. It is simply to assert that their way of life and many of their beliefs are very different from our own.

As Popper (1972) and Lakatos (1970) have argued, the inferential process underlying experimental method is a simple one known as *modus tollens*. If one proposition implies another that turns out to be false, the first proposition is inferred to be false. Formally, *If A then B, and not B, then not A*. Levi-Strauss (1966, 13–14) points out that the development of neolithic cultures depended on the painstaking method of trial and error, which is but a practical expression of *modus tollens*, and much the same point could be made about palaeolithic people in their development of flint technology. *Modus tollens* is but one formal expression of the principle that beliefs and opinions cannot fly in the face of reality. If a belief implies a proposition that is not true, it must itself be rejected. It is hard to see how humanity could survive without respect for this principle of reason in those areas that directly concern the practical necessity of gaining a livelihood (cf, Bloch, 1975). The possession of fields of vocabulary peculiar to a particular contextual rationality might tell us that one language is more suitable than another for certain purposes and activities. It is misleading to say that language 1 is deficient in comparison with language 2 for this reason. All languages express the culture and interests of their users in the development of vocabulary and enthymemic reasoning. It is only a misleading way of expressing this point to say that all languages are deficient in relation to one another in some respect or other.

Logical distinctions will find *some* expression in the grammar of a language. It would otherwise be hard to see how they could be made at all. But one can only claim that such and such a grammatical construction is the only way of making a logical distinction if no other way can be found to do so. It would, for example, be absurd to maintain that the French do not understand the distinction between mass and countable objects because "beaucoup" and "combien" both express what we would express by "a lot of" and "many" in one case and "how much" and "how many" in the other.

Nor would it be justifiable to maintain that a language that did not contain the interrogative or imperative moods did not allow the expression of commands or questions. This can be done in other ways, through the use of the indicative mood. A language that lacks a rich array of subordinate constructions will still be able to express, say, causality;

"When the window was hit by a stone, it broke."

can be expressed by

"A stone hit the window. It broke immediately."

The second example uses an active rather than a passive construction. This does not prevent it from expressing the idea of something happening as a result of an event.

Those who, like Honey, wish to claim that some languages or dialects are fundamentally less developed, or differently developed in relation to others, need to show that language 1, say, lacks *any* way of expressing a distinction that language 2 expresses. He cites A. Bloom (1981), who writes: "In studying Japanese one is forced to recognize that what one had lazily assumed to be fundamental categories of human thought are merely local habits" (quoted in Honey 1983, 11).

An example is unfortunately not given, but it is worth drawing attention in this connection to Potts (1971), who points out that the predicate calculus, the artificial language that maps out the formal logical principles of generality, can also be used to express these concepts as they occur in Japanese (Potts 1971, chapter 14, p. 10). Honey does go on to mention another example given by Bloom:

> Actual examples of the intellectual consequences of specific languages are now being offered by the American scholar Alfred H. Bloom, who has produced evidence suggesting that educated Chinese speakers tend not to entertain certain kinds of theoretical speculation because their language does not contain the grammatical construction that would allow them to do so. (Honey 1983, 11)

Bloom is here claiming that Chinese speakers have difficulty in understanding and engaging in counterfactual reasoning. Counterfactual reasoning is a form of reasoning that proceeds from premises known to be false in order to examine the consequences of what would have been the case if they had been true—for example, "If Hitler had won the Battle of Moscow . . . " or "If I were to win the lottery . . . ." Bloom refers to the alleged *difficulty*, not *impossibility*, of the Chinese being able to do so. In fact Bloom shows how they can provide a grammatical alternative for the expression of counterfactual thoughts in everyday contexts, as well as more theoretical ones, through such devices as stating what we would state by

If China had gone through that stage then . . .

by

China did not go through that stage. But if it had, then . . .

In other words, although not accustomed to using certain constructions, the Chinese are not prevented from expressing certain kinds of thought, albeit in a slightly different way from the way in which Europeans and Americans would.

To conclude this chapter, the Platonic "different types of mind" claims of verbal-deficit theory have been shown to be empty. Although logically possible, the kind of evidence that would be appropriate to such claims has nowhere been produced. Neither has the evidence been supportive of the idea that high-variety users are better than low-variety users in reasoning ability or, indeed, that there *exist* high or low varieties in the relevant sense. The fact that verbal-deficit theorists have disconnected their model from the hereditarian claims of the mental testers has left their theories open to a much wider variety of interpretations, including some of a Rousseauist or Marxist character. I will turn to these questions in the next chapter, for they have direct implications for educational practice.

CHAPTER 10

The educational implications of the verbal-deficit controversy

Like I.Q. theory, verbal-deficit theories have had an enormous impact on educational theory and practice. However, because the verbal-deficit movement is more diffuse, the educational results have been more varied and ambiguous. However, there was nothing ambiguous about the early claims of some of the verbal-deficit theorists, and it is salutary to be reminded of some of them as this is the form in which they were—and still are—often most influential at a popular level. We have already seen how psychologists like Bereiter and Engelmann decided to treat certain children as if they did not possess a language. Their "academically oriented pre-school program" (see also Blank and Solomon 1969) proceeded on the assumption that certain nursery-class children needed to learn the basic elements of English.

Bernstein, not making such large claims, writes quite categorically of the education of the lower working class in a way that is highly reminiscent of the educational prescriptions of I.Q. theory (see Chapter 5). It is evident that at this stage in the evolution of his thought there remained a deterministic bias and a pessimism about the possibility of change:

> Their time span of attention will be brief and this will create the problem of holding and sustaining attention. They are not interested in following the detailed implications of a concept or object and the matrix of relationships which this involves; rather they are disposed towards a cursory examination of a series of different things. (Bernstein 1961b, 164)

This lack of attention and curiosity leads to learning difficulties:

> This is by no means to say that a *public language* speaking pupil cannot learn. He can but it tends to be mechanical learning and once the stimuli cease to be regularly reinforced there is a high probability of the pupil forgetting. In a sense, it is as if the learning never really gets inside, to be integrated into the preexisting schemata. In fact it looks as if this is so, for unlike the *formal* language oriented pupil, the *public* language pupil lacks these receptive schemata or if he possesses them they are weakly organized and unstable. (Bernstein 1961b, 174)

These difficulties become particularly apparent at the secondary stage, according to Bernstein. It is worth remarking that it has become fashionable to deny that Bernstein ever had anything to do with verbal-deficit theory, to the extent that Atkinson is able to write:

> In retrospect it is, perhaps, just as well that Bernstein did not draw on Piaget explicitly: commentators blind to the structuralist style of thought would have assimilated them both to equally crude views on developmental psychology. Formal analogies, for instance, between the public/restricted in Bernstein and the Piagetian concrete and the equivalent homology of the formal/elaborated and the formal would no doubt have confused the issue for just too many. Interpretations of linguistic deficit would probably have been combined with equally crude notions of the development of thinking and intelligence in children and adolescents. (Atkinson 1985, 59)

It is salutary to be reminded of what Bernstein actually wrote:

> Although the pupil may pass the primary stage without a great sense of unease, the discrepancy between what he is called to do and what he can do widens considerably at the secondary level. It becomes increasingly analytic and relies on the progressive exploitation of what Piaget calls *formal* operations, whereas working class pupils are more likely to be restricted to *concrete* operations. (Bernstein 1961b, 165)

In other words, lower-working-class children are arrested at a certain level of intellectual development and are unable to make the transition from context-dependent to context-independent forms of thought, which is essential for the proper possession of a human type of constitutive rationality. Bernstein even remarks that the problems of educating working-class children need to be thought out as though middle-class children did not exist (Bernstein 1961a, 306). This is clear enough. In some ways the strong version of verbal-deficit theory is even more strongly Platonic in character than I.Q. theory, as it makes very firm distinctions between different kinds of minds. I.Q. theory actually finds this idea harder to conceptualize: I.Q. scores constitute a continuum of achievement, rather than a series of sharp breaks—although we should remind ourselves of Jensen's attempts to distinguish between level 1 and level 2 types of intelligence (see Chapter 4).

Like low I.Q. scorers with level 1 intelligence only, restricted-code users will benefit from formal, mechanical types of learning rather than discovery methods:

> A major dilemma confounds the education of the lower working class pupil. Unlike the middle class pupil, he lacks the understanding of basic concepts, neither is he oriented to building his experience on those concepts. Insightful generalization is difficult. His order of cognitive evaluation would indicate that drill methods are required so that the elements for later conceptualization are gained. Although this is unfashionable, I suggest that where the culture induces a relatively low level of conceptualization, association rather than

gestalt learning in children is more efficient. . . . The passivity of the pupil makes him peculiarly receptive to drill methods, but resistant to active participation and co-operation. The teacher requires techniques such that these elements are gained without prejudicing later generalization. Because formal relationships are difficult for the child to perceive (relative to the middle class child), the tendency is to make the context of teaching very concrete. (Bernstein 1961a, 306)

As well as advocating a limited curriculum and formal teaching methods for working-class children, Bernstein was also prepared to make quite specific curricular recommendations for working-class children—for example, in the teaching of reading, where he advocates phonic rather than look-and-say methods (Bernstein 1961a, 313), and mathematics, where he thinks that an approach using problem-solving techniques that require logical ordering before arithmetical calculation can take place will provide major difficulties (Bernstein, 1961a, 305).

Without the hereditarian bias of I.Q. theory, linguistic determinism was not so firmly rooted. If working-class pupils could be isolated sufficiently from their home background, then their linguistic performance could be significantly improved. This was the assumption behind the American programs already referred to, and it was realized in Britain through a project reported on by Gahagan and Gahagan, entitled "Talk Reform."

In this project, children selected as "linguistically deprived" were given a language remediation program designed to make their use of language more explicit. For example, one of the materials developed by Gahagan and Gahagan was a set of cards called "Picture Stories," which was designed to enhance children's ability to give a context-free description. A similar exercise was called "I-am-the-teacher" and was used with various materials, such as a toy farm. The Gahagans state:

> The children worked in pairs, facing each other across two desks which have been put together. A screen is placed between them so that they can talk to each other but neither can see what the other is doing. Each child is given an identical set of materials which can be assembled. One child assembles his materials first. When he has completed his task, he has verbally to instruct his partner to produce an identical assembly. He is not allowed to show him. The other child can ask questions but must not look at his partner's assembly. When it is finished the two must compare to see whether the *instructions* have produced similar arrays. (Gahagan and Gahagan 1970, 47)

I will comment on the educational value of such exercises shortly. We have looked at the assumption s on which they have been based and found them to be erroneous. The effects of verbal-deficit theories on the education systems of a number of countries have, however, been incalculable. To take Britain as an example, they found acceptance in the Plowden Report of 1967 (cf. Plowden 1967, 1:119) and later again in the Bullock Report on English (Bullock 1975). Bullock states: "There is an indisputable gap between the language experience that some families provide and the linguistic demands of the school situation" (Bullock 1975, 54)

Certainly, the effect of verbal-deficit theories on primary and nursery education has been profound. Very often strong statements of verbal-deficit theory, such as those of Bereiter and Engelmann have been taken as conventional wisdom by teachers (cf. Gordon 1978, Gordon 1981). Tizard and Hughes write: that "So strong is the belief in a working class language deficit that some teachers have been incredulous of our findings, arguing that in *their* schools children arrive 'barely able to talk'" (Tizard and Hughes 1984, 159).

The result of these beliefs is that working-class children are often given a compensatory education that they do not need. Much of what has gone on and still goes on under the name of language development is, therefore, of very dubious educational value indeed:

> Our analysis of the educational role of the nursery school admittedly runs counter to current beliefs. Many politicians and professionals believe that nursery school stimulates intellectual growth and language development, and gives socially disadvantaged children a head start in school. There is very little British research evidence to substantiate these claims. Certainly this study suggests that children's intellectual and language needs are much more likely to be satisfied at home than at school. (Tizard and Hughes 1984, 256).

Before considering whether there is *anything* worthwhile in the development of spoken language in schools, we need to consider the evolution of Bernstein's position. It has been noted that in some respects Bernstein retained his view that the codes distinguished between different levels of rationality or even between rationality and the lack of it (e.g., Bernstein 1973c, 205–6). On the other hand, Bernstein was prepared to admit increasingly that working-class children could on occasion produce elaborated (i.e., "high") variants. I have already noted in Chapter 8 that this tendency to equivocate produced less rather than more coherence in the theory.

A most striking instance of this is the way in which Bernstein appears to have changed his views as to the educational implications of his theory. In an article entitled "The Myth of Compensatory Education" (Bernstein 1972), he writes: "If the culture of the teacher is to become part of the consciousness of the child, then the child must first be in the consciousness of the teacher" (Bernstein 1972, 225).

Bernstein also asserts, in the same article, that the speech system that results from a restricted code is not linguistically deprived (Bernstein 1972, 224). Actually this is not a formal contradiction of his previous position, as he employs at this stage the special Chomskyan concept of competence that is quite consistent with a performance-based deficit. In this sense, competence is a form of neurological encoding of gramatical rules, rather than a disposition manifested in linguistic performance (cf. Winch 1985b for a fuller explanation of this point), but there is no doubt that there is an apparently bewildering *volte face* here. Writing of the kind of education that he thinks is appropriate for working-class children, Bernstein argues:

> Many of the contexts of our schools are unwittingly drawn from aspects of the symbolic world of the middle class, and so when the working class child steps into school, he is stepping into a symbolic system which does not provide for him a linkage with his life outside.
>
> It is an accepted educational principle that we should work with what the child can offer: why don't we practice it? The introduction of the child to the universalistic meanings of public forms of thought is not compensatory education—it is *education*. (Bernstein 1972, 225)

There is certainly a Rousseauist flavour to these statements. The child's inability to respond to school stems from a failure of society in general and teachers in particular to appreciate the value of working-class culture, rather than to failures within that culture itself. It might be asked uncharitably, as does Rosen (1974), whether or not Bernstein himself contributed to such a lack of appreciation, particularly in the light of the remarks quoted above.

It might still be questioned to what extent Bernstein's position has really changed. He still wishes, for example, to introduce children from the working class to "universalistic meanings of public forms of thought," implying clearly that working-class culture lacks some of the essential attributes of rationality. The qualification that the working-class child is not "in the technical sense linguistically deprived" that is, in the psycholinguistic but not the performance-based sense, (Bernstein 1972, 222), makes one wonder how much has changed or, at least, how clearly the thesis has changed.

One can go further than merely suggesting that language development based on deficit-theory programs are a waste of time. They may, quite unintentionally, actually do some harm. One of the most disturbing features of the Tizard and Hughes study of four-year-old children attending nursery is that working-class children who appeared lively and inquisitive at home, appeared withdrawn and monosyllabic in the nursery:

> The working class girls in our study were particularly affected by the nursery school setting. In their relations with the nursery school staff they tended to be much more subdued, passive and dependent than at home. The staff responded to this perceived immaturity of the working class children by

pitching their talk to them at a lower level. Far from compensating for any
inadequacies in their homes, the staff were in fact lowering their expectations
and standards for the working class children. The overall effect was that
working class children already appeared to be at an educational disadvantage.
(Tizard and Hughes 1984, 256–57)

For various reasons the working-class children felt a greater social
unease in the informal, low-key, child-oriented setting of the nursery.
"Informal interview" types of linguistic encounter with adults, whose
purpose is not clearly understood by the child and also (to some extent)
by the teacher either, reinforce this sense of unease on the part of the
children, which is in turn misinterpreted by the adult professionals as a
sign of linguisic deficit. The point is tellingly made by the authors when
they quote a conversational exchange from Tough (1977b):

TEACHER: Tell me what is happening, will you?

CHILD: That's a farm.

TEACHER: Oh, that's a farm here is it? Who lives in the farm, I wonder?

CHILD: Them lot (points).

TEACHER: Oh, who are they?

CHILD: The people.

TEACHER: What sort of people live in a farm? (child shrugs) What do
we call a man who lives in a farm, do you know?

CHILD: Farmer. (Tough 1977b, 64)

Tough cites this exchange as an example of "the difficulty that many
children have in taking part in conversation" (Tough 1977b, 64). Tizard
and Hughes comment:

At no point does Tough consider the possibility that Paul's limited contribution
to this conversation might reflect his social unease or defensiveness, rather
than his limited grasp of language, or suggest that the teacher might learn from
listening to his conversation in an out of school setting, or by transforming the
social situation between teacher and child. (Tizard and Hughes 1984, 258)

This is very much the point that Labov made fifteen years earlier with
respect to the findings of American educational psychologists about
urban black children. Verbal-deficit theories can easily become a form
of self-fulfilling prophecy. The child who is "deprived" is seen to be in
need of "linguistic enrichment." When the child fails to respond, the
appearance of deficit is confirmed.

Tizard and Hughes do make some positive suggestions. They point
out, for example, that a greater awareness on the part of teachers of what

the children are capable of at home with their parents would greatly help them with their work at school. They draw attention to the natural curiosity of young children and to their wish to learn more about the world around them. Middle-class children, they suggest, are given a greater store of general knowledge by their mothers than working-class children. They believe that this may be related to their generally higher score on the Stanford–Binet I.Q.test:

> The Stanford–Binet test for this age contains mainly language items, for example, moving objects in pictures, and asking such questions as "Why do we have houses?" "What is a chair made of?" Although usually considered part of general intelligence, high scores depend on the extent of the child's vocabulary and general knowledge, as well as her grasp of more basic verbal skills, such as understanding the concept "different." Children's I.Q. scores may also be affected by other factors such as the extent to which they understand the tester's intentions, and their ease and motivation in a test situation (Tizard and Hughes 1984, 156).

This observation is interesting for two reasons. I.Q. scores do not give an indication of a child's basic linguistic ability or basic ability to reason, provided that they are functioning reasonably well on the test. At this level they are more likely to give an indication of the child's general knowledge and vocabulary. This, of course, is far from showing what the proponents of I.Q. testing claim that the tests show, and the above remarks also point to the importance of cultural and motivational factors in achieving a good score. It also suggests that nurseries and infant schools might profitably consider answering children's questions and responding to their desire for information, rather than asking them questions whose point or content they do not properly understand.

Bernstein's suggestion that the teacher must be conscious of the culture of the child is certainly pertinent. But what it should mean is this: children need to be given credit for their linguistic abilities and curiosity. They need to be given a chance to develop knowledge and skills relevant to the larger concerns of society as well as to their own subculture. If Bernstein and others had actually looked at the language of working-class children in its proper context, then exhortations such as his own would have been less necessary.

I have suggested that working-class language is not *cognitively* deficient, but have not shown that it is not *socially inappropriate* for certain purposes. It is most important to distinguish between these two claims, for they have very different educational consequences. In attacking the proposition that "all languages are equally good," Honey (1983) confused these two issues. The harmful educational consequences of belief in verbal-deficit theories have already been noted. Does it follow that nonstandard dialects, styles, and accents are suitable for educational purposes? It does not seem to follow. The argument put forward here has supported the proposition that working-class language is not cognitively deficient. That does not mean that it is either socially acceptable or appropriate in certain educational and occupational contexts. Larry's style of address and vocabulary would not, for example, get him very far in conversation with a teacher or chargehand.

Some linguists have advocated that nonstandard dialects should not be interfered with in children's spoken language, because children are at ease with their dialect and any attempt to change it will cause insecurity and resentment. Children should be given the opportunity to write in Standard English for certain purposes such as correspondence, application forms, and reports, but there is no reason why they should not write in their own dialects when they are writing stories or even examinations. Trudgill (1975) is a prominent exponent of this *bidialectal* approach.

This view is fiercely attacked by Honey on the grounds that the social convention that Standard English is used in many situations to speak and write is an important sociolinguistic fact that, if ignored, will place nonstandard users at a disadvantage:

> For schools to foster nonstandard varieties of English is to place their pupils in a trap. To persuade such speakers that their particular nonstandard variety is in no way inferior, no less efficient for purposes of communication, but simply *different* is to play a cruel trick. (Honey 1983, 21–22)

Honey does his case no service by mixing up the *cognitive* and *social* aspects of adequacy. We have already seen that the *assumption* that nonstandard varieties (empirically associated with "low" varieties in the cognitive sense) are cognitively deficient can lead to harmful educational consequences. On the other hand, it may well be wrong to persuade children that their nonstandard variety will be just as efficient for purposes of communication in all contexts as a standard variety might be. It is not hard to see that Larry's nonstandard variety will not endear him to teachers and employers. Labov is, in fact, well aware of this:

> Larry is one of the loudest and roughest members of the Jets, one who gives the least recognition of the conventional rules of politeness. For most readers of this paper, first contact with Larry would probably produce some fairly negative reactions on both sides: it is probable that you would not *like* him any more than his teachers do. Larry causes trouble in and out of school; he was put back from the eleventh grade to the ninth, and has been threatened with further action by the school authorities. (Labov 1969, 193)

Honey is quite right to point to the sociolinguistic fact that certain styles and dialects are more efficient than others for gaining access to education and employment. He does his case no good, however, by conflating it with the verbal-deficit thesis. This consideration also shows us why well-meaning sociolinguists like Trudgill have got it wrong. It cannot be demeaning to a person to point out that his dialect or style is unlikely to bring about certain things that the person desires or finds valuable. This is quite a different matter from telling him that his variety of language is a poor vehicle for rationality.

Under current social conditions, there is nothing to be gained from pretending to children that certain styles and dialects of written English will help them when in fact they will not. It is a pity that this simple point has been confused with the much wider and muddier issue of verbal-deficit theories by both protagonists and antagonists of the bidialectal approach. An essentially simple Rousseauist point about minimizing the social barriers to personal achievement has got confused with a near-Platonic view that there are different type of mentality, hierarchically ordered, expressed in different forms of the same language.

The approach of persuading children to change their language in order to achieve educational success and occupational mobility may not succeed. It may be that deep-rooted factors of motivation, culture, and interest need to be considered as well. Is there *any* sense in which we can speak of the development of spoken language at school that does not lead to educational practices that are damaging at worst and time-wasting at best? There is scope for the development of certain speaking and listening abilities in a way that does not presuppose a deficit on the part of children, but that seeks to extend their *expertise* in certain kinds of use of language in certain contexts. This does not contradict the views expressed in this book. It does not follow from the fact that a language is adequate for communication and the fact that speakers can make perfectly good use of it as a vehicle of practical and theoretical rationality, that their expertise in the use of that language cannot be improved in certain contexts and for certain purposes.

There may be a lot of scope for improving children's ability to listen. It may also be valuable for older primary children to discuss a particular topic in groups, thus encouraging listening, turn-taking, putting forward one's views in a nondogmatic fashion, summarizing the important points, and reporting results. It is encouraging to note in this connection that the documents putting in place the national curriculum in the United Kingdom (i.e., Kingman 1988, Cox 1988), do not make any use of the deficit model but treat the development of spoken language in the manner described above. One scheme that might seem suitable for such a purpose is de Bono's Cort Thinking (de Bono 1976). A difficulty here is that the non–subject-specific character of this scheme, designed to promote practical reasoning skills independent of subject matter, is based on a dubious assumption that context-free thinking skills can be easily transferred (an assumption challenged, for instance by McPeck 1984, Winch 1987). The development of communication skills may, however, be a desirable by-product of such a program. The question arises whether such group discussion work might not fruitfully be developed in a subject-specific manner, for example, in science or environmental studies in the primary school and in history, geography, and social studies in the secondary school.

Whether such work is desirable or possible will very much depend on curricular decisions taken within subject fields. However, the improvement of communication skills of the sort mentioned would be a desirable by-product of such an inquiry-based approach if it could be justified as a learning strategy for a particular subject matter. There is some evidence from the curriculum documents for the United Kingdom national curriculum that such an approach is being adopted in a range of subjects.

Cooper and Honey are right to point out that the cocksure and opinionated approach of such as Larry is not necessarily to be recommended as a communication technique for all occasions. However fluent a logical thinker we may feel him to be, it is also clear that a willingness to listen, to take turns, and to express one's point of view in a tentative and nondogmatic fashion are desirable communication objectives and should be developed, where appropriate, in school. Bernstein may have been wrong to think that "I mean . . . " and "I think . . ." are markers of any deep level of rational thought. Indeed, these expressions may, at times, be little more than idioms or matters of style. On the other hand, the signaling of an open mind or the willingness to listen to another opinion may be very important, not just for the impression that other people get of one, but also because of the attitude of mind that it develops in a young person, an attitude that will prove to be of value in adult life.

The encounter with more formal styles of exposition may well prove to be quite difficult for some students, but will also have a beneficial effect for them in clarifying ideas and techniques of expression. The critical and logical skills of active listening can also be usefully developed in such a context as a fairly formal group discussion, not to mention a sympathetic understanding, which seems, for example, to be absent from Labov in his assessment of Charles.

With all the interest that there is in the development of spoken language, we must not lose sight of the fact that schools exist to a very great extent for the promotion of literacy and of knowledge based on the acquisition of literacy. It is to this important subject that we must now turn.

CHAPTER 11

Literacy, literate culture, and education

It is a curious fact that the important part in educational achievement played by becoming literate is so neglected in psychometric and verbal-deficit theories. The strangeness of this omission is made greater by the way in which literacy has been held by many to mark a significant divide between different levels of rationality.

Very often, the distinction made by Lèvy-Bruhl between logical and prelogical thought is taken over and used to explain the difference in modes of thinking between literate and nonliterate cultures. Such a case can be found, for example, in Stubbs (1980) and Olson (1977). It is no exaggeration to say that the divide between the literate and the nonliterate is seen by some scholars as marking a cognitive divide as great as that opened up by strong forms of verbal-deficit theory. Stubbs, for example, writes:

> It is arguable that the logical mode of thought embodied in syllogistic reason- ing could only develop in practice once propositions could be written, set against one another, read and re-read and contradictions and consequences noted. (Stubbs 1980, 105–6)

A similar although more cautious approach can be found in Goody (1977) and Goody and Watt (1962). However, Olson (1977) goes so far as to identify literacy with assertoric uses of language, that is, uses of language concerned with truth and falsity. Spoken language, however, he associates with "simple communication:"

> In written text, the logical and ideational functions become primary, presum- ably because of the indirect relation between reader and writer. The emphasis, therefore, can shift from simple communication to truth to "getting it right." (Olson 1977, 278)

Olson argues that speaker's meaning depends on the intentions of the speaker together with contextual clues as to those intentions. Sentence meaning, on the other hand, is relatively independent of context, being dependent on the meanings of the words composing the sentence. Sen- tence meaning is primarily associated with writing, speaker's meaning with speech (Olson 1977, 277–78). In advancing these arguments, Olson is in effect saying that constitutive rationality depends on the development of writing, for if speech cannot properly express truth-telling or assertoric uses of language, then it is inadequate for giving and assessing evidence, reasoning, or argument, and so for any level of constitutive rationality. These are very large claims, indeed, and, if vindicated, would more than justify Honey's contention that some forms of language are more efficient than others as they employ a literary medium.

However, it is fair to say that elsewhere in his article Olson makes claims that are less strong. Stubbs's point, too, is ambiguous, oscillating between the idea of writing as giving access to any form of logical thought and the idea that the formal development of theoretical reason only became possible with the advent of literacy. Thus he writes: "Without writing, science and history are inconceivable, since at one stroke writing overcomes the limitations of human memory" (Stubbs 1980, 104). This is a weaker claim, for if logical thought could not be expressed in speech, neither could any sort of rationally based subject like science or history. Olson, too, is prepared to state: "Truth in oral utterance has to do with truth as wisdom. A statement can be true if it is reasonable, plausible, congruent with dogma or the wisdom of elders; truth is assimilability with common sense" (Olson 1977, 277).

There is a certain amount of position-changing evident in these remarks, and it may well stem from a confusion on the part of the authors themselves as to exactly what claims they are making. The strongest claim, that literacy is necessary for any sort of constitutive rationality, is clearly implausible. Writing can render explicit and permanent what in speech is context-dependent and impermanent (that is, speech needs a context to be understood in very many cases). Therefore, writing is obviously very useful for all kinds of purposes but does not transform a language from a nonrational to a rational mode of communication.

In order to make this claim stick, it would be necessary to show that certain words and constructions were simply not available in spoken language but were available in writing (cf. Chapter 9) and this has not been done. Another fall-back position, also stated by Olson, is that argumentation in speech is not, properly speaking, logical reasoning, for it is usually disjointed, implicit, and reliant on enthymemes (Olson 1977, 273). Are we prepared to accept that the use of enthymemes is not, properly speaking, a species of logical reasoning? We have already seen how important a sympathetic interpretative context is to the proper understanding of informal reasoning. Hawkins attempted to show how working-class children used a more context-dependent form of speech than middle-class children. The implication of this was that context-dependent speech was a less rational mode of communication than relatively context-independent speech. He did *not* show that, when the occasion arose, working-class children were incapable of speaking in a context-independent manner, and, in fact, Edwards, as we have noted, presented evidence to suggest that, when the need was perceived, working-class children could elaborate and decontextualize their speech. Enthymemes and contextual clues are employed in everyday talk; one can assume that their uses and limitations are understood by speakers. There is no evidence to suggest that this is not the case, and Olson does not present any. Just as when the objects referred to in speech are present in the physical context, reference to them becomes unnecessary, so when common premises are understood and accepted, explicit reference becomes unnecessary as well.

Literacy, then, does not affect the scope of constitutive rationality. Does it have any cognitive effects? The argument developed here suggests that there are no necessary effects that follow from the acquisition of literacy. What effects there are will be of a practical nature. There is no *logical* necessity for cognitive effects to follow from the acquisition of literacy (cf. Finnegan 1973, 1982).

These effects will be to improve, in certain contexts, the quality of theoretical and practical reasoning. It is no longer possible to distinguish between literate and completely nonliterate cultures, except in a very few cases. Even the functional and social specialization of literacy in a pure form is a rarity and is taken up as a test case for the study of the possible cognitive effects of literacy (e.g., Scribner and Cole 1978, on the Vai people of Liberia).

Within Western society most people are to some extent literate, but there is a tremendous range of literacy that is distributed in different ways throughout the social classes (cf. Hoggart 1957). Literacy encourages social differentiation and awareness of cultural and educational differences. It is also affected by the division of labor, which may encourage the development of certain specialized notations—for example, in mathematics and music.

Developments of rationality in society as a whole are almost always the by-product of the development of a group or even an individual manipulator of the literary medium. The development of tables and the use of abbreviated notation was greatly aided by the invention of the alphabet, as Goody (1977) has pointed out. Techniques deriving from tabular representation, in particular the use of specialized notations, provided a great boost to the formal development of theoretical reason and mathematics. The development of logical notation, stemming from the work of Frege, Wittgenstein, and others, is an important example of this. Here again literacy proved to be an enabling factor in a very specialized academic environment, although its indirect effects on social and technological development were considerable—for example, through the application of truth-table notation to the electronic design of computers.

In terms of practical reasoning, the relative permanence of writing, a feature of the earliest systems, gave a new memory aid and a method of sequencing tasks (through the use of lists) that proved to be a great help not only to governmental administration, but also to many kinds of tasks requiring a store of knowledge and a carefully planned sequence of activity. Here again, the earliest forms of literacy enabled certain types of practical reasoning tasks in specialized situations to be better undertaken.

Is literacy necessary to develop what is sometimes called "critical rationality," that is, the capacity to adopt an objective and critical attitude toward authoritative statements? (cf. Winch 1983). It is certainly true that skepticism and, indeed, some form of experimental method exist in traditional societies. What the permanence and suitability for private contemplation of writing seem to have enabled is the development and *persistence* of critical and skeptical lines of thought among *groups* of individuals. The way in which writing permitted the reproduction and accumulation of critical thought may have been a decisive factor in the development of critical rationality.

What about the development of specific contextual rationalities? Here again it is easy to make sweeping claims such as, for example, that nonliterate societies do not have a proper literature (a claim discussed and criticized by Finnegan 1973). On the other hand, permanence gives a potentially vast memory aid to its users, and this, together with the property of *surveyability*—that is, the property of being able to be taken in as a *whole*—permits the ordering and sequencing of tasks. Scientific, technological, and administrative activities could all benefit from these possible effects. History, as opposed to historically oriented myth, benefited from the availability of an aid to memory that was not changed and adapted to current needs as is often the case with speech.

There is no doubt that literacy has enabled the vast growth of a greater range of activities, as well as the genesis of new ones, but this has not been an inevitable result. The development of literacy is not a homogenous process. It tends to be socially specialized, and among literates there are degrees of ability and specialized developments of certain literate techniques. Literacy seems to be a necessary condition rather than a cause of certain sorts of cognitive development. Even here, the necessity is practical rather than logical. Literacy cannot transform the categories of human constitutive rationality, although it may enable them to be codified and systematized for specialist study. Literacy may help the specialized development of theoretical and practical reasoning ability.

There is no justification then for regarding nonliterates as suffering from a species of linguistic deficit. What nonliteracy may well restrict, however, is access to a wide range of profitable and satisfying activities that are available in a modern society. This in itself justifies the central place of reading and writing on the primary school curriculum, as these skills provide a key to the acquisition of many of the other skills and knowledge necessary for success in a complex society.

Some might argue that this does not matter and that minority subcultures should be allowed to live in their own thought world unsullied by the demands of industrial society. Whatever arguments might be raised in favor of the belief that radically different cultures from our own may have different forms of constitutive rationality (a view known as relativism), they are not especially applicable in this case. Such a view may have some apparent plausibility when applied to the comparison of cultures very different from each other—for example, the modern United States and the aboriginal cultures of Australia—but it strains credulity when applied to different groups within our own society, which will, in most cases, share a common language. Keddie, for example, chides Labov for trying to show that Black English Vernacular can be reduced to the same pattern of reasoning as Standard English, when really it expresses a different logic altogether (Keddie 1973, 9–10). She does not attempt to show how the logic of Non-Standard English is a different logic from that of Standard English. If this were true, it would be difficult to communicate at all with many other groups in our own society, which is surely an absurd conclusion. Relativism, therefore, does not present a convincing argument for not teaching literacy to all the children in our society.

It is also claimed that the rise of electronic media has made the need for literacy obsolete. Audiovisual technology, it is claimed, will render the printed word unnecessary for successful life for people from nonliterate backgrounds (c.f. Postman 1973). Accordingly, schools need no longer teach literacy to those who will not want or require it in their adult lives. It is far from clear, however, that electronic media are making the printed word obsolete. It is true that they have played a part in orienting the teaching of modern languages more towards a preoccupation with spoken rather than written competence. This is a welcome development, one that was assisted by audio recording and is perhaps an area where in the past there has been an overemphasis on literary skills. But in a more general way, electronic media have contributed to making more information, both audial and printed, available to society.

Computers, video displays, microfiche, and other inventions provide new ways of storing and processing print that in themselves require new paraliterary skills to handle. In addition, the new inventions rely on older literary skills for their employment. More generally, the introduction of such technology has led to rapid social and economic change and to a corresponding need for a workforce that can change with it. It is hard to see how the increased flexibility and adaptability that will be required from people, will lessen rather than considerably increase the need for literacy.

My conclusion, then, is that literacy permits the development of contextual rationalities and is continuing to do so at a time when the "information revolution" is giving rise to different ways of storing and processing the printed word. Literacy, far from becoming obsolete, is becoming even more pervasive in many activities and walks of life. It is, however, the contextual aspect of rationality that is, above all, developed by literacy. Literacy does not permit a "crossover" to higher forms of constitutive rationality or between different *kinds* of constitutive rationality.

Why, then, is the acquisition of literacy sometimes such a problematic matter in schools? The answer to this question comes in three parts. The first part is that, as already noted, many groups have got by with a minimal acquaintance with the literary medium. It has played a relatively marginal part in their culture and in their employment and has not been essential for successful living.

The second part of the answer is that both the acquisition and the use of literacy are a far more private matter than the acquisition and use of spoken language. The difficulty and unfamiliarity of reading and writing, unlike the participatory process of talking, is often a painful matter for some children, who never really come to grips with the new memory, perceptual, and motor skills that are required by reading and writing. This is not to say that there is *no* social or participatory side to learning to read, but it is to say that it plays a much less important role than it does in the case of learning to speak, where social interaction is a *logical* rather than merely pedagogical requirement of successful learning.

The third part of the answer relates to the second. Although the acquisition of new skills is essentially a *preliminary* to communication with literary media, the point of the exercise is all too often not perceived by some children at school, and children from nonliterate home backgrounds will not pick it up at home either. Wells (1981, 1987) reports from the Bristol longitudinal study that although there are no significant social class differences in the acquisition and use of spoken language, there *are* significant social class differences in educational achievement, and these correlate with differences in social class acquaintance with and attitudes toward literacy.

Schools, although they exist in large part to teach literacy, are not themselves in certain ways very suitable institutions for literate communication, and this applies particularly to primary schools. They are relatively small, and spoken communication is therefore more effective. As self-enclosed institutions they do not have, at least as far as the children are concerned, any strong links outside the school, and there is little need for out-of-school literacy communication. The hectic and busy atmosphere of a primary school working day is not conducive to the leisurely contemplations of books, which is one of the main rewards of reading. Schools, especially primary schools, are themselves as institutions unsuited for everyday written communication. The implications of this paradox will be further explored in Chapter 13.

These remarks do not constitute the basis of yet another argument for "deschooling society." If the point is a good one, and the nature of school can, to a degree, be inimical to the acquisition of literacy, then there are serious implications for the organization and the curriculum of schools, particularly with regard to reading and writing. If children are to practice genuine as opposed to artificial communication tasks, then they will need to do so in situations where literate communication not only has a definite advantage over oral communication, but can also be seen to be meaningful and enjoyable. Schools also need to become places where the enjoyment of reading and writing is more possible than at present. These considerations imply a greater coordination among schools themselves and between schools and other institutions than exists at present (although the introduction of a national curriculum is inaugurating a long period of great educational change in the United Kingdom that may result in such coordination). It also implies a practical turn to the literacy curriculum, where the emphasis is more on communicating to acquire useful abilities and knowledge rather than an emphasis on the acquisition of literacy as merely a *preliminary* to communication and enjoyment. There are signs of a growing awareness of this implication, both in the movement to provide more interesting reading material for children and in attempts to provide communication-oriented writing in the primary school. It is worrying, however, that many of those educators taking such steps, who are also influenced by psycholinguistic theory, seem to think that there are no formal skills to be taught in the acquisition of literacy (cf. Hall 1988; Waterland 1988).

These considerations imply far-reaching changes in school organization, particularly in the de facto autonomy that schools possess in developing their own curricula with relatively little regard to the world outside school. In Chapter 13 the view will be developed that the position taken on literacy in this chapter implies a greater local and national say in organization and development of the curriculum than has hitherto existed in the United Kingdom and the United States.

CHAPTER 12

Equality, culture, and interest

In this chapter, a critique will be offered of both Platonic and simplified Rousseauist-Marxist explanations of different levels of educational achievement. An alternative view of the phenomenon will be offered, based on the argument advanced in Chapter 3, one that compensates for the inadequacies of the Rousseauist-Marxist position.

The argument put forward in Chapter 6 was that the concept of intelligence that I.Q. theory depended on did not, ultimately, do justice to our everyday conceptions of human ability. In particular, it was argued, the idea of a natural ceiling on ability was mistaken, as was the notion that there exists a *general* quality of natural ability independent of the particular activities and contexts in which an individual endeavors to succeed.

The hereditarian claims of I.Q. theory were not discussed, as they were essentially empirical rather than conceptual matters. The alleged fraud that surrounded the work of Burt alerted many people interested in this field to the fact that forces greater than intellectual curiosity were at work. In particular, it has been urged, the need to supply an *ideology* that *legitimated* the current system of society was a strong motivating factor behind the persistent attempts of psychometric theorists to provide a justification for an unequal state of affairs in the ordering of society (e.g., Blum 1978).

What does this claim mean? The term *ideology* is used in different senses, but I will use it in the Marxist sense of such writers as Althusser in this particular context (cf. Althusser 1971, Althusser 1972). In this sense, an ideology is a system of ideas and beliefs with a certain internal coherence. An ideology can be contrasted with a *science* because it does not ultimately derive assent to its propositions from test and experiment, but from various nonrational forms of persuasion including fraud and a reliance on rhetorical devices rather than logical argument. The success of an ideology may depend on its appropriateness to the requirements of the age and on the fact that it appeals to and draws on the folk beliefs of uneducated people whose support it recruits (cf. Gramsci 1976). There have been several Marxist critiques of I.Q. theory along these lines (e.g., Simon 1976, Blum 1978), and there is certainly some reason to think that there are ideological aspects to psychometry.

Apart from the evidence of fraudulent practice and the more general accusations of dubious scientific methodology, there are other features of the theory that lend weight to the accusation. One is the refusal to recognize the conceptual difficulties that exist in making intelligence a single, discrete attribute of an individual. Another is the persistence with which tests are taken to measure this quality, despite the mounting evidence that success in them depends on general knowledge, practice, linguistic ability, and so on. Despite evidence that success on I.Q. tests is related to test-taking ability, and hence to quite specific forms of intellectual achievement especially relevant to educational success, it is persistently claimed that they measure a general intelligence factor. Blum (1978, chap. 7) however, cites a number of studies that show weak or no relationships between I.Q. and occupational success, but a strong relationship between educational success and occupational status (cf. Vroon 1980, 62–67, for more evidence of this nature).

The strong relationship between I.Q. and test-taking ability might explain the connection between I.Q. scores and educational success generally. The absence of a strong relationship between I.Q. and subsequent occupational *success* as opposed to *status* might be explained by the weak relationship between test-taking abilities and the abilities required in various high-status occupations. In other words, test-taking ability might be a necessary condition for achieving high occupational status. It is not, however, a *sufficient* condition for success in a range of high-status occupations.

An ideology *legitimates* a certain organization of society because it provides a justification for the rise and maintenance of, for example, capitalism. According to Blum, the emerging bourgeoisie needed an ideology that would, in the first place, justify their own activities in becoming the dominant social class and thus displacing the older feudal elites. In the second place, the hereditarian aspects of the theory would justify the permanence of the new order of things to those of the emergent working class, who might otherwise be tempted to believe that they merited a controlling role in society (cf. Blum 1978, chap. 12, for a development of this argument).

Similar considerations have been advanced in relation to verbal-deficit theories (e.g., Rosen 1974, Dittmar 1976), but it is far less clear that these theories can play quite the same legitimating role as I.Q. theory, for they do not have a hereditarian component. This does not mean to say that verbal-deficit theories do not constitute an ideology. Although they may lack the clear legitimating function of I.Q. theory, it can be said that they provide an agreeable refuge for lazy thinking about educational achievement, providing educationists, administrators, and politicians with a convenient and sterotyped view of a complex problem and an easily understood means of "pigeonholing" pupils according to popularly held views about social class and language use.

If however, the Platonic view of the relationship between ability, social class, and educational success cannot be sustained, it does not follow that the Rousseauist-Marxist account gives a completely coherent picture either. There may be elements of truth in it, but it certainly does not follow that it constitutes the whole of the picture. We saw in Chapter 3 that certain important facts about human nature might be helpful in understanding the relationship between social class and educational achievement. The attachment of people to a familiar background of community, interest, and custom was, it was suggested, important in understanding why and how people develop the potential they have in the way that they do.

The difficulties with the Rousseauist-Marxist view can now be made clearer. According to this approach, the two elements that work to secure the continuation and acceptance of the social order are the overt or threatened use of force (cf. Lenin 1917) and fraud—that is, the propagation of false ideas about the way in which society actually runs and is organized (e.g., Marx and Engels 1846). More sophisticated versions of the theory put more weight on the persuasive element, especially when considering advanced societies, and also play down the fraud element, tending more to emphasize the internal coherence of the ideology, the way in which it fits in with the spirit of the time, its popular intelligibility, and even its success in apparently giving a satisfactory explanation of certain social phenomena (cf. Gramsci 1976).

The Platonic view of educational achievement, enshrined in I.Q. theory and some versions (the "strong" ones) of verbal-deficit theories, gains its hold in educational circles and in the popular imagination through the apparent rigor of its empirical investigations and the way in which it appears to correspond to popular ideas—for example, that there are some people who are cleverer than others and are born that way, or that certain varieties of language are incapable of expressing coherent thought. Finally, such ideological views about educational achievement provide a *rationale* for the allocation of scarce resources to those who will benefit most from them—that is, the relatively privileged sections of society—and in this way claim their allegiance to the ideology. This is the Rousseauist-Marxist account of how Platonic legitimating ideology works in the area of educational ideas.

A telling consideration against this account, even in its sophisticated, Gramscian versions, is that Platonic legitimating ideology has enjoyed a relatively limited amount of success at both the popular and the intellectual levels. It had a period of success by contributing to the system of secondary selective education put into place in the United Kingdom after the Second World War, but debate and dissent, as well as the rise of a more egalitarian and democratic consensus in the decades following that war have led to a loss of influence for I.Q. theory as a comprehensive explanation for educational achievement. At the most, it can only be held that psychometry enjoyed a period of influence in important sectors of the educational and political establishment as well as holding some grip on the popular imagination, but this influence was constantly under challenge.

A more general variant of the Gramscian argument might be deployed at this stage. General political and social inequality, of which inequality of educational achievement is an important feature, are maintained, to a large degree, by what is called a *hegemonic* system of ideas, that is, a system of ideas that is dominant throughout the society. These ideas are disseminated at a variety of levels from the most sophisticated philosophical systems to popular folk conceptions about how society should be run. Such a complex network of ideological beliefs give rise to essentially false *ideas* about sexual and racial inequality, the reality of equal educational opportunity, and the possibility of achieving justice through political reform, according to this explanation (cf. Boggs 1976).

The most sophisticated versions of the legitimating ideology argument are, ultimately, a dressing up of the classical Marxist argument of conspiracy to fraud. Even if the fraud being perpetrated has a certain internal coherence, uses the trappings of serious empirical inquiry in its defence, and can point to important matters of fact to support it, it is still a fraud, albeit a clever and subtle one. Nor does it matter that those who propagate such ideas believe them wholly or only to a certain extent. If the ideas are largely false and have been largely arrived at by nonrational means then the authors themselves are the victims of self-deception and the agents of a largely unwitting fraud perpetrated on the general public.

However, the Rousseauist-Marxist position requires something like this argument if it is to be maintained in its pure form, and this proves to be its undoing. If all members of society were equally rational practical and theoretical reasoners, they would quickly realize the injustice and disadvantage of the system of unequal access to opportunity and reward if they were among the deprived groups. As such groups do not take the opportunity to correct this state of affairs (the working class, in the Marxist sense being numerically by far the largest group in advanced Western societies, should not have too much difficulty in doing this), there must be some factor preventing their realization and elimination of injustice. This is where the concept of a legitimating ideology acquires its explanatory value.

But now a paradox appears. If the assumption of broad natural equality is correct, then it should be ascertained by anyone endowed with a reasonable level of theoretical rationality. But then why do some people notice that this natural equality is not being realized in social arrangements while the vast majority do not notice? The usual answer is that some people, the future political élite of the working class, are possessed of a special sort of insight into the nature of society and how it should be changed to achieve real equality. This insight, often called the science of Marxism-Leninism, allows this elite to propose and initiate action on behalf of the working class. Leninist versions of the Marxist position usually develop this conclusion in a quite explicit way (cf. Lenin 1917, Althusser 1971, Althusser 1972).

But this argument shows that the original assumptions are undermined if certain social facts about a rough equality of rationality are called into question by the view that a certain élite has a better insight into things as they really are than does the mass of the working class. The theoretical rationality of the working class is deficient if its members are unable to work out or discover the disparity between natural and social inequality, and its practical rationality is deficient if an élite is required to lead its members to success in achieving social and political equality.

The Rousseauist-Marxist position then emerges as a form of Platonism, whereby an educated élite discover the mismatch between natural equality of ability and social inequality of treatment and of achievement, and put themselves at the head of a working class unable to discover and correct the situation for itself. The Platonism that emerges when this argument is thought through is, admittedly, nor a very strong version. The élite need only be better at theoretical and practical reasoning than the nonélite, not necessarily superior in I.Q. or constitutive rationality. In this connection, it is interesting to note that there are Marxist thinkers who see the reality of verbal deficit as an instance of the bourgeoisie's domination of the working class (e.g., Hoare 1975). The conditions of social and working life that capitalism imposes on workers, according to this further argument, are intellectually and linguistically debilitating enough for the rationality of the working class to be somewhat impaired. Both this and the original, more general argument, however, imply that on its own the Rousseauist-Marxist view is difficult to sustain and needs supplementing.

On the other hand, certain elements in the position are not wrong. We have seen no good reason to doubt, for example, that there is not some rough kind of natural equality in human ability, expressed in a common structure of constitutive rationality. Neither I.Q. nor verbal-deficit theory has given us serious reason to doubt this assumption. What the Rousseauist-Marxist position overlooks is that although it may be true to some degree that small differences in natural ability are socially transformed into large differences in economic, political, social, and educational achievement, it does not follow that people would necessarily have a practical interest in forcing a great change. Large numbers of people might realize the facts of great differences in achievement and even perceive them to some extent as injustice on an abstract level, but might still not have an overriding reason for bringing about a swift change in social organization.

There could be a number of reasons for this. Someone might recognize the injustice but still reckon that, for him personally, any change would make for less efficiency and result in a worse outcome than would adherence to the status quo. He may see the inequality, but reckon that too much disruption of his own life and that of his family would result from attempts to bring about change. He may simply have a greater interest in getting on with his own life in his own family, workplace, and community. Most people do not entertain vast personal, social, or economic ambitions and prefer to retain their attachment to familiar surroundings, customs, and ways of life. Finally, someone might opt for gradual reform so as to reconcile the desire for greater social equality with the desire for a reasonably quiet life. The development of politics in the United Kingdom, for example, points to this type of solution. Naturally, there are exceptions, and ambitious members of the working class exist who have large social, political, economic, or educational aspirations. But such people tend to be the exception rather than the rule, in most communities.

The abilities of people tend to be shaped in ways marked out by their community, culture, and economic life. The formal fact of equal educational opportunity may suggest wider possibilities, but for many children and their parents these possibilities are difficult to perceive on anything other than a fairly abstract level, as they do not go with the grain of their own experience and interest. The peculiar demands made by reading and writing are often difficult to relate to the easily understood rules and conventions of verbal communication. The relatively context-independent nature of the processes, the need for practice and trial and error and their comparatively solitary nature, tend to make literacy a difficult medium in which to achieve expertise, particularly when one's own culture does not especially use or value literacy in day-to-day leisure and work or, at least, uses it in fairly limited and marginal ways (cf. Hoggart 1957).

It does not seem surprising that such devices as I.Q. tests, related as they are to the ethos of schooling and literacy, should differentiate between social classes in this way. Neither is it surprising that verbal-deficit theories should have arisen to explain the facts of different levels of educational achievement. The different demands of literacy and speech also distinguish different cultural habits and interests. Ways people have of maintaining their communal identity, such as the use of dialect, accent, and so on, can often become confused with deep differences in ways of thinking. Bernstein did not help with this matter when the few examples of restricted code that he did give came in nonstandard dialect (e.g., Bernstein 1965, 158; Bernstein 1964, 59).

Where, then, does this leave notions of natural equality? In the first place, we can say with reasonable confidence that among normal, healthy humans there is the same degree of constitutive rationality, that is: all people, whatever their sex, social class, race, or culture, share a very similar logical and conceptual structure for thinking about and acting in the world. This does not mean that there are not large variations in ability in all sorts of different activities among different people. But we can understand these important facts about human nature without resorting to the Platonic "different kinds of minds" conception or to the simplistic social arguments of the Rousseauist-Marxist variety. The inadequacies of the latter form of explanation make it easier to take seriously the culture-interest argument first advanced in Chapter 3, particularly in relation to the arguments of the previous chapter concerning literacy.

It makes sense to say, in general terms, that people can be compared in ability in particular activities, and that sometimes we can point to superior *natural* abilities of one kind or another as factors explaining their success, as opposed to interest, motivation, or particularly good coaching. For example, A might have a high degree of manual dexterity, B might have a capacity for careful reflection, C might be naturally observant, D socially perceptive, and so on. Certain exceptional individuals possess more than one and sometimes several of these gifts, and they will stand out as naturally very able people. Another person may, by dint of exceptional application and persistence, transform a mediocre natural aptitude into an outstanding talent. There is no harm in talking about natural abilities, if one is prepared to do so in ways that are fairly specific and subject to some criteria of truth or falsity that could be established empirically.

There is, however, not much sense in making hypothetical judgments as Vernon (1950) does, saying that *if* so-and-so developed an interest in football, for example, he would be better at it than most people who are now playing it because of his high I.Q. score. It is difficult, if not impossible, to provide a convincing test for this particular kind of counter-factual and hence it lacks any clear meaning. If motivation, interest, and cultural background are very important in the development of an ability, then there can only be limited clues as to how a person might develop given his or her lack of interest, motivation, and encouraging cultural background. So judgments to the effect that certain people or groups of people are intrinsically more capable of creative writing or mathematics than others, let us say, when they come from widely differing backgrounds of interest and opportunity, amount to very little, as there is no clear way in which they could be tested. Of course there are circumstances in which we will want to say unequivocally that someone has an outstanding natural talent and is able to develop it in unpromising circumstances. Cases such as that of Ramanujan, the Indian mathematician with little formal training in the subject, who produced many important results and became a Fellow of the Royal Society before dying in 1920 at the age of thirty two, come to mind. But in these cases we are confronted with clear, categorical, and unmistakable evidence that someone has a specific talent. It would in general, however, be wise to refrain from the making of sweeping statements unless we are confronted with clear and unmistakable evidence, or unless we are comparing like with like in terms of similar backgrounds and interests.

We have arrived at a basic, working notion of equality of ability in the sense of a shared kind of constitutive rationality, and we have been able to build on it an idea of the diversity of natural and acquired abilities at particular activities. We have also seen that it is possible to make comparisons between people in terms of ability, provided that we are properly comparing like with like. We have also noticed that it can make sense to talk of an outstanding natural ability that can transcend an unpromising environment, provided that we are given clear evidence of such a thing.

The sort of judgment that we need to be extremely wary of is the case where like is not compared with like or where the judgment is hypothetical and it is not clear what kind of evidence could support it; for example, "If John hadn't been interested in the classics, he would have made a brilliant footballer"—where the boy in question had never shown any interest, did not persevere with an activity he was not interested in, and so on, although he might have scored well on an I.Q. test.

In the light of this discussion, the notion of equality becomes a rough-and-ready guideline for the provision of educational opportunity. For although there is a rough equality of ability among people, there is a tremendous diversity in ability (both natural and acquired) and interest in a whole range of different activities and occupations. When this diversity has a certain cultural patterning, this notion of rough equality (in terms of constitutive rationality) can sometimes be very difficult to realize in specific activities where there may not be a tradition of interest and concern in that culture or community.

Consider, as an example, the provision of tuition in classical music in two communities—one where there is a tradition of listening and playing in many families, and one where no such tradition has existed before. It is likely that, in general, ability to appreciate and to perform classical music will tend to flourish more readily in the first community than in the second. None of the above considerations should suggest for one moment that *material* inequality does not contribute to differences in educational achievement. By this I mean such factors as poverty, poor housing, and poor conditions of public health. Clearly, these should be minimized in order to make equality of educational opportunity as much of a reality as possible. All that I suggest is that there comes a point at which one has to recognize and come to terms with individual and social diversity, and that provision must be made within the resources available to a society to develop this diversity to the benefit of both individuals and society itself.

Ultimately, the question to what extent educational achievement is brought to some level of *approximate* parity between different social groups and, indeed, between individuals becomes a question of political and social priorities concerning the allocation of resources. For example, to what extent should certain childrens' ability in music be deliberately developed by the allocation of resources that might otherwise be diverted to children with learning difficulties? The notion of equality of achievement will, in practice, have to be tempered by specific choices as to priorities in the allocation of educational resources.

CHAPTER 13

Conclusion

In this chapter I will make a positive comment on the theories that have been discussed and on their implications. I will suggest that our education systems can be developed in such a way that, while we can accept the distinction between theoretical and practical rationality, we are not thereby committed to the Platonic view that the former is necessarily superior to the latter and should always get priority of resources and esteem. This is not to doubt or to fail to recognize the enormous advances in human understanding that have been brought about by the theoretical approach.

We have, however, already noted that not all cultures and not all individuals can be expected to share in or to wish to develop a purely theoretical outlook, particularly in fields of inquiry distant from their own everyday concerns and those of their community. Historically speaking, the theoretical pursuit of knowledge has been the preserve of educational and cultural elites who have very often deliberately excluded a large part of the population from their interests, interests that a vast majority of the population would have been disinclined to share anyway. Historically and sociologically, the theoretical attitude to the pursuit of knowledge and understanding has attracted prestige and esteem to a far greater extent than the practical attitude to knowledge and understanding.

This development, inevitable and desirable as it may have been on a world-historical scale, poses severe problems for a society that genuinely wishes to provide a mass education within the constraints of a democratic political system. The difficulty consists in interesting those subcultures and groups whose concerns are, to a large extent, nontheoretical in becoming involved in an enterprise distant from their own preoccupations, particularly if successful participation is likely to mean adapting to a culture and way of life somewhat different than the one they currently enjoy. It was argued in Chapter 3 that the human desire to preserve identity and to gain esteem as part of a familiar culture and community is not to be underestimated.

There is at the present time much debate about how to interest children from those sections of society that have traditionally failed to take full advantage of what a formal education has to offer. There are a number of reasons for this new concern. A modern society needs to mobilize all its talents in order to maintain its position as a trading, commercial, and manufacturing success in a very competitive world. Technological innovation and scientific advance change patterns of employment very rapidly and lead increasingly to the need for a well-educated and adaptable population that can cope successfully with such change. In some countries, a large increase in leisure time through unemployment or early retirement, which are the accompaniment of economic upheaval, have also been felt to require solutions that depend on the development of increased educational opportunities.

It is very often said that those changes that ought to be made to an education system in coping effectively with this need to involve more children entail a more practically minded approach to the curriculum. What is needed, it is held, is an educational approach that will appeal to the interests and aptitudes of a section of the population traditionally excluded from a profitable and enjoyable experience of education. In themselves, these are not views with which I would seek to disagree. In particular, if such changes mark a move away from the drill and rote learning techniques advocated by psychometrists and some verbal-deficit theorists, they should be welcomed. If they herald a departure from the secondary assessment that separates the educational haves from the have-nots purely on the basis of performance on a theoretically oriented curriculum, this is also to be welcomed.

What I wish to argue for positively are two points, each closely related to the other. The first is that theoretical and practical approaches to the curriculum need not be mutually exclusive: in fact, they need and complement each other right from the earliest stages. The second point is that providing the right combination of approaches to the curriculum in different areas of subject matter with different pupils at different stages of educational development is likely to be a complex and difficult matter, one not easily achieved by a piecemeal approach.

Something of the nature of the problem can be seen at the earliest stages of education, where the ability to read, write, and perform written calculations requires, as numerous commentators have remarked (e.g., Donaldson 1978), a certain theoretical attitude towards language. That is, the writing system has of necessity to be mastered as a set of rules, conventions, and procedures to a certain extent independent of the uses to which it will be put. We learn our native language by example and participation without the need to gain an explicit mastery of formal rules and procedures. At the earliest stages of writing, however, a child is faced with the need to learn the sound system in a fairly abstract way, and to acquire a working concept of sentences, words, and letters, as well as the complexity of spelling rules, to name just a few of the theoretically based ideas involved in the acquisition of literacy.

And this is just the beginning of the technical accomplishments needed to become literate. Literacy is a tool of communication, and one paradox of mass education is that this point is to some extent lost because of the conditions under which education takes place. A school, although a task-oriented institution, is different from other task-oriented institutions in one important respect. Much if not all of the work carried out in school is undertaken as a preparation for life outside school and can therefore serve only as rehearsal for it. Much of the work that goes on in schools is therefore not oriented towards practical goals, and this institutional feature fits easily with the theoretical attitude toward knowledge and understanding that is cultivated in many schools.

The idea that education is a preparation for adult life is fostered for many children in the way of life of their parents and their parents' habits and interests. For example, children see that literacy can be valuable and enjoyable from the way in which their parents gain their livelihood and enjoy their leisure. They also get the message that being literate is essential to self-esteem in their section of society. These factors help to compensate for the difficulties that learning to communicate and understand without being able to do so *meaningfully* must give to many children. The very institutional nature of schools leads to a situation where the point or purpose of writing activities is difficult for some pupils to grasp.

The reasons for this state of affairs are bound up quite intimately with the way in which schools are organized and run, and it is this that makes the idea that literacy is for effective communication often so difficult to get across. Stubbs puts the point well:

> With reading and writing, it is difficult to provide children with tasks which have genuine purposes, especially in the early stages. Requiring children to read aloud, for example, often has no genuine communicative function, although it is unavoidable as a teaching technique and check for the teacher. Similarly, it is difficult to provide a genuine audience for a child's writing, for the simple but awkward reason that genuine institutional writing has only an abstract audience which is difficult, if not impossible to simulate in a classroom. At any rate, the traditional classroom task of "writing an essay" may in some ways be more difficult than the task performed by professional writers, since it may involve writing without clear stylistic conventions, with no genuine communicative function, and with no genuine audience in mind. (Stubbs 1980, 115)

Stubbs sums up neatly the difficulties inherent in any institutionally based teaching of literacy. The problems spill over into most other subject areas, as the presentation of knowledge in school is usually in written form with no clear audience in mind, no established stylistic conventions to follow, and—most important—no genuine communicative function. The state of mind that the acquisition of knowledge and abilities is not primarily for a practical purpose, but as an end in itself, thus tends to be acquired and reinforced in the minds of many children. This matters particularly to those children who do not realize the benefits of literate communication within the life of their own cultural group.

There are no easy or glib ways of getting around what is a major paradox of mass education,—namely, that it is a preparation for life that divorces itself from life in order to be an efficient preparation for it. But it is perhaps time to consider how children whose abilities are not fully exercised at school may come to benefit more from the system. Once again, consideration of literacy provides a key to understanding a lot of the problems.

Learning the basic conventions of reading and writing cannot have any immediate relevance to a very young child. But, very soon, some communicative pay-off should appear, and, in good primary school practice, it does. A five- or six-year-old gains the satisfaction of seeing his or her own experience put into writing for others to read and admire, or he or she may gain employment from being told or even reading a simple story. Becoming literate is a lengthy process, and the question remains as to how this early progress can be sustained. Because of its very nature, the written medium works best for communication between people who are not in each other's immediate spatial or temporal context, and although there are situations that may arise within a school— for example, writing up a project to display to the school, entering stories for a competition, or writing letters to one's parents or to pen pals—the very physical nature of a small school will limit the number of opportunities of this kind.

One is led to the conclusion that any major effort to improve the communicative content of literacy learning in schools will have to lead to the problem being posed and resolved on a supra-school basis, at the level of a local, state, or even national authority. Piecemeal efforts by individual teachers or schools are, by the nature of the problem outlined, hardly likely to make much of an impact. It would be natural to see a serious attempt to construct a communicative literacy curriculum as something that would involve the skills, efforts, and insights of teachers but also lead to a program that had them surrender some of their control over what goes on in the classroom in the interests of a more widely based and coordinated program of work. Such considerations have far-reaching implications for the distributed autonomy of teachers, principals, and school boards such as is found in the United States and Britain. The work would need to be planned at a level higher than that of the individual school. Resources such as libraries, museums, nature trails, study centers, urban farms, and so on would need to be allocated and used properly.

The United Kingdom has already begun to go down this route with the passing of the Education Reform Act of 1988. This has control of the curriculum and provisions for the assessment of children's performance on it rest with the Secretary of State of Education. Financial resources, however, are to be further devolved to schools, so that initiatives for the coordination of resources will have to come from them to a very large extent. As these reforms are just coming into effect at the time of writing, it is at present difficult to tell whether the combination of curriculum centralization and financial disaggregation will actually work to provide an efficient allocation of educational goods, particularly of those items that are too costly to be funded by individual schools.

The content of the curriculum specifies three "core" subjects: science, mathematics, and english and a further seven "foundation" subjects, technology, history, geography, music, physical education, art, and a modern foreign language. All primary school children—that is, five- to eleven-years olds, will undertake the program of core subjects and most of the foundation subjects, and will be expected to reach certain attainment targets at certain stages of their education. Crosscurricular work will not be ignored, and so, for example, some of the attainment targets in English will be realizable in other areas of the curriculum, by writing a report as part of technology project, for instance. In this way, it is envisaged that the curriculum will receive a more practical orientation, with an emphasis on the meaningful employment of communicative abilities.

The provision of a greater range of communicative contexts can be bettter served by a national system of coordination (it remains to be seen whether or not the British model will successfully provide it), and the inclusion of science, technology, and art as compulsory subjects gives greater scope for the development of curricula more oriented to the development of practical rationality. A national curriculum also provides a basis for what Hirsch has called "cultural literacy,"namely a common core of knowledge and understanding that provides both a sense of national identity and ready access to effective further learning through the application of essential background knowledge to the acquisition of new material (Hirsch 1987, Hirsch 1989).

It will be argued that such proposals are yet another attempt to implement an instrumental approach to education and a vocationalism that is tied to the business of "wealth creation." Some would even argue that these proposals introduce a new form of Platonism into the education system. The élite will continue to receive a traditional, theoretically oriented education in private schools or special "centers of excellence," while the great mass of children will follow a program oriented towards the practical concerns of industry and commerce. As A. O'Hear states:

> The majority, though, will be left to fend for themselves in the "world of work," cut off from anything that industrialists might find useless or subversive. This would be educational and political Platonism with a vengeance, save for the fact that (as Lord Young constantly reminds us) the new men of

gold are in the main untouched by academic education. But their children will not be, and so, despite the barbarism of those actually piloting our industrial ships, the educational division of the country into two classes of men and two cultures will be perpetuated. (O'Hear 1985, 147)

The centralizing consequences of the ideas outlined in this chapter will be taken as proof that a practical tilt to the curriculum is merely a camouflage for the real aim of bringing education more directly under the control of the industrialists and the "wealth creators." What can I reply to such hypothetical accusations? There are arguments in ethics and political philosophy for a fairly centralized education system, but consideration of these arguments goes beyond the scope of this book. I have merely made out a practical case based on the desirability of giving more children more satisfaction and value out of schooling than they receive at the present time. The charge of Platonism can be refuted in the following way.

We saw in Chapter 2 that making a distinction between theoretical and practical aspects of rationality is itself to a large extent a matter of convenience. Very often, theoretical and practical approaches intertwine with and complement each other. In the days when traditional crafts were still well-established, it was possible to make a clear distinction between the theoretically oriented education that a young man studying "Greats" at Oxford might receive and the apprenticeship of a wheelwright. In the modern world, theory and practice are usually not sharply separable in this way. Theoretically acquired knowledge is used in technological innovation, and practical discoveries are used, for example, to construct equipment for the testing of experiments in the "pure" area of a subject. A child who hopes to pursue a practical or technologically oriented career cannot hope to do so without the acquisition of literacy and numeracy, and the trade or occupation that they may choose to pursue will itself depend on theoretical knowledge. Here Gladwin's contrast between the navigational techniques of the Trukese and those of the Europeans suggests nicely the kind of interdependence between theory and practice that has come to exist in the modern world, although, in many areas, the practitioners are likely to take a more flexible and innovative attitude to the theory than Gladwin suggests would be the case with European navigators.

If these considerations are valid—and if the arguments put forward in this book concerning the need to harness ability to interest in order to develop it properly are also valid—then it is possible to see theoretically and practically oriented curricula as no longer mutually exclusive. In primary education, the work has to be practically oriented to a considerable extent, in order to give the children some idea of its point or purpose. Where this does not happen, children from literate backgrounds may well understand this through the lives of their parents and communities, while those from nonliterate backgrounds may largely fail to do so.

This does not mean that skill and practice should be all and knowledge of facts of no account. These different aspects of learning are not mutually exclusive; skill and practical ability require a certain amount of *knowledge* in most cases, while the *acquisition* of knowledge requires, in many cases, a background of skill and practical know-how. Hirsch is right in pointing to the importance of a core of fairly general knowledge in order to build up conceptual structures in more specialized subjects. He is right also to point to the importance of knowledge in the acquisition of the ability to read and listen with understanding, although this is more of a logical and epistemic necessity than it is a psycholinguistic one as he maintains (Hirsch 1987, chap. 2). If, for example, I am to understand atomic structure on the basis of an analogy between the orbits of the planets round the sun and of electrons round an atomic nucleus, it is a necessary condition of my reading or listening to this information with any significant degree of understanding that I understand what orbiting involves in the example of the sun and its planets.

The advocate of a more practical approach to education need not remain on the defensive about his *aims* for education either. There is no incompatibility between liberal aims for education and a practical direction to that education, if liberal aims are conceived of in terms of the development of independence and greater understanding of the world, rather than merely acquaintance with a cultural heritage. The fact that an education may have a vocational use need not disqualify it from having a liberal function as well. The fact that I learn skills and acquire knowledge that result in my making a living through selling something marketable does not render my education of only vocational value. No one would think of saying this of a young man or woman who went to art school and succeeded in making a comfortable living creating sculptures or paintings. There is no reason to suppose that a person who makes artifacts or provides services of less obvious prestige or high cultural status has thereby forfeited all claim to have enjoyed the liberalizing aspect of education thereby. Liberal–vocational, like theoretical practical, is a false dichotomy, one that limits the range of what we can offer to develop the talents of all our children.

This point is being seen to some extent by the British national curriculum designers. The working group on design and technology (Parkes 1989) suggests, for example, that work-related activities can foster and demonstrate the value of personal qualities, including the ability to work constructively with others, a spirit of enterprise and self-discipline and a sense of social responsibility. To which one might add that designing and making artifacts can increase a sense of aesthetic awareness, enlarge an awareness of what solutions to problems are possible and desirable and develop an expertise in the solving of those problems. These seem to be legitimate aims of a liberal style of education, ones perfectly applicable to practical education, if this is conceived of and designed in a broad and generous way.

A further development of practically oriented education in the United Kingdom has been the establishment of City Technology Colleges for older pupils who are motivated toward and wish to pursue a more practical and technologically oriented secondary education than is normally available in the comprehensive schools. This is a welcome revival of interest in the dormant British tradition of high-quality technical education, but, paradoxically, the requirement that the City Technology Colleges should follow the National Curriculum may inhibit their effectiveness. A major weakness in the emerging British national curriculum reform is that it is, in some ways, too narrow. There is not enough scope for differentiation at the secondary level. A core primary curriculum will ensure a basic level of knowledge, skill, and understanding that all pupils should be able to share. But there is no good reason why children and adolescents should not be able to develop educationally in a more explicitly practical or vocationally oriented way after the age of fourteen if they and their parents wish them to do so. A National Curriculum that fails to motivate large numbers of older children will not constitute much of an educational reform and will ensure the loss of many of the benefits that could be gained by such an upheaval in a national system of education. A national curriculum that aims to benefit all children should be seen as a tree with a common trunk out of which several broad branches grow.

If anything, the theme of this book is the need to go beyond rigid distinctions between theoretical and practical understanding and to provide the beginning of a conceptual map for appreciating both the underlying equality of human potential and the vast diversity of its realization in the interaction of culture, interest, and community that occurs in a modern, complex society. It might even be said that those who complain about the tendency toward more practically oriented curricula betray their own continuing attachment to the Platonic hierarchy of knowledge for its own sake as the only sort of knowledge of any real value, followed below by practical knowledge and understanding, which are of a purely conditional order of value—valuable only insofar as they allow the work of theoretical reason to be carried on.

Bibliography

Abbs, P. 1987. Training Spells the Death of Education, "The Guardian." 5/1/ 87.

Althusser, L. 1971. *Reading Capital.* London: New Left Books.

———— 1972. *Lenin and Philosophy.* London: New Left Books.

Atkinson, P. 1985. *Language, Structure and Reproduction: An Introduction to the Sociology of Basil Bernstein.* London: Methuen.

Bennett, J. 1964. *Rationality.* London: Routledge.

Bereiter, C., and Englemann, S. 1966. *Teaching Disadvantaged Children in the Pre-School.* Englewood Cliffs, N.J.: Prentice Hall.

Bernstein, B. 1958. Some Sociological Determinants of Perception. In Bernstein 1973a, 43–61.

———— 1959. A Public Language: Some Sociological Implications of a Linguistic Form. In Bernstein 1973a, 62–77.

———— 1960. Language and Social Class. In Bernstein 1973a, 78–86.

———— 1961a. Social Class and Linguistic Development: A Theory of Social Learning. In A. H. Halsey, J. Floud, and C. A. Anderson, eds., 1965, 288–314.

———— 1961b. Social Structure, Language and Learning. *Educational Research* 3: 163–76.

———— 1962a. Linguistic Codes, Hesitation Phenomena and Intelligence. In Bernstein 1973a, 92–111.

———— 1962b. Social Class, Linguistic Codes and Grammatical Elements. In Bernstein 1973a, 112–37.

———— 1964. Elaborated and Restricted Codes: Their Social Origins and Some Consequences. In J. Gumperz and D. Hymes, eds., 1964, 55–69.

———— 1965. A Socio-linguistic Approach to Social Learning. In Bernstein 1973a, 138–164.

———— 1971. A Sociolinguistic Approach to Socialization with Some Reference to Educability. In Bernstein 1973a, 165–92.

———— 1972. A Critique of the Concept of "Compensatory Education." In Bernstein 1973a, 214–26.

———— 1973a. *Class, Codes and Control,* vol. 1. London: Paladin.

———— 1973b. *Postscript to Paladin Edition of Class, Codes and Control,* vol. 1. In Bernstein 1973a, 257–78.

———— 1973c. Social Class, Language and Socialization. In Bernstein 1973a, 193–213.

Bernstein, B., ed. 1973d. *Class, Codes and Control,* vol. 2. London: Paladin.

Blackburn, S. 1984. *Spreading the Word.* Oxford: Blackwell.

Blank, M., and Solomon, F. 1969. How Shall the Disadvantaged Child be Taught? In A. Cashdan, ed., 1972.

Blishen, E. 1978. *Sorry Dad*. London: Hamish Hamilton.

Bloch, M., ed. 1975. *Political Language, Oratory and Authority in Traditional Society*. London: Academic Press.

Block, N., and Dworkin, G., eds. 1977. *The I.Q. Controversy*. London, Quartet.

Bloom, A.J., *The Linguistic Shaping of Thought*. New Jersey: Erlbaum.

Blum, J. 1978. *Pseudoscience and Mental Ability*. London, New York: Monthly Review Press.

Boggs, C. 1976. *Gramsci's Marxism*. London: Pluto.

The Bullock Report 1975. *A Language for Life*. London: H.M.S.O.

Burt, C. 1949. The Structure of the Mind. In S. Wiseman, ed., 1973, 115–40. Revised by the author.

———— 1955. The Evidence for the Concept of Intelligence. In S. Wiseman, ed., 1973. 182–203. Abridged and revised from the original by the author.

Cashdan, A., ed. 1972. *Language in Education*. Milton Keynes: Open University Press.

Cooper, D. 1984. Labov, Larry and Charles. *Oxford Review of Education* 10, no. 2: 177–92.

Cox Report 1988. *English for Ages 5 to 11*. London: H.M.S.O.

de Bono, E. 1976. *Teaching Thinking*. London: Penguin.

Dittmar, N. 1976. *Sociolinguistics*. London: Arnold.

Donaldson, M. 1978. *Children's Minds*. London: Fontana.

Edwards, A. D. 1974. Social Class and Linguistic Inference. *Research in Education* 12: 71–80.

———— 1976. Speech Codes and Speech Variants: Social Class and Task Differences in Children's Speech. *Child Language* 3: 247–65.

———— 1980. Teaching Styles and Communicative Disadvantage. Paper presented to the British Education Research Conference, September 1980.

Eysenck, H. 1973. *The Inequality of Man*. London: Fontana, Temple Smith.

Finnegan, R. 1973. Literacy Versus Non-Literacy: The Great Divide? In R. Horton, R. Finnegan, eds. 1973.

———— 1982. Orality and Literacy: Some Problems of Definition and Research. Delivered as a public lecture, Australian National University, Canberra, August 1982.

Furth, H. G. 1961. The Influence of Language on the Development of Concept Formation in Deaf Children. *Journal of Abnormal and Social Psychology* 63: 386–89.

———— 1973. *Deafness and Learning: A Psychosocial Approach*. Belmont, Calif.: Wadsworth Publishing Co., Inc.

Gahagan, D., and Gahagan, G. 1970. *Talk Reform: Explorations in Language for Infant School Children*. London: Routledge.

Galton, F. 1892. The Classification of Men According to Their Natural Gifts. Excerpts from *Hereditary Genius*. Chapter 3, pp. 14–38, 2d. ed. London: MacMillan. In S. Wiseman, ed., 1973, 25–36.

Giglioli, P. P., ed. 1972. *Language and Social Context*. London: Penguin.

Ginsberg, H. 1972. *The Myth of the Deprived Child*. New York: Prentice Hall.

Gladwin, T. 1964. Culture and Logical Process. In N. Keddie, ed. 1973.

Goody, J. 1977. *The Domestication of the Savage Mind*. Cambridge: Cambridge University Press.

Goody, J., and Watt I. 1962. The Consequences of Literacy. In P. P. Giglioli, ed., 1972, 311–357.

Gordon, J.C.B. 1978. *The Reception of Bernstein's Sociolinguistic Theory among Primary School Teachers*. Norwich: University of East Anglia Press.

―――― 1981. *Verbal Deficit*. London: Croom Helm.

Gramsci, A. 1975. *The Prison Notebooks*. London: Lawrence and Wishart.

Grandy, R. 1973. "Reference, Meaning and Belief." *Journal of Philosophy* 70, n. 14: 439–52.

Gumperz, J., and Hymes D. 1964. *The Ethnography of Communication*. American Anthropologist Special Publication, vol. 66.

Hall, N. 1988. *The Emergence of Literacy*. London: Hodder and Stoughton.

Halliday, M.A.K. 1978. *Language as Social Semiotic*. London: Arnold.

Halsey, A. H., Floud, J., and Anderson, C. A., eds. 1965. *Education, Economy and Society*. (London: Collier-MacMillan).

Hawkins, P. R. 1969. Social Class, the Nominal Group and Reference. In Bernstein 1973d, 81–92.

―――― 1973. The Influence of Sex, Social Class and Pause Location in the Hesitation of Seven Year Old Children. In Bernstein 1973d.

―――― 1977. *Social Class, the Nominal Group and Verbal Strategies*. London: Routledge.

Hearnshaw, L. S. 1979. *Cyril Burt, Psychologist*. Ithaca, N.Y.: Cornell University Press.

Herrnstein, R. 1971. I.Q. *Atlantic Monthly*, September.

Hirsch, E. D. 1987. *Cultural Literacy: What Every American Needs to Know*. Boston: Houghton Mifflin.

―――― 1989. Education: The Primal Scene. *New York Review of Books*, March 2, 1989. Vol. XXXVI, no. 3, 29–35.

Hoare, Q. 1975. Education: Programmes and People. In Hoyles, ed., 1977, 33–54.

Hoggart, R. 1957. *The Uses of Literacy*. London: Chatto and Windus.

Honey, J. 1983. The Language Trap. Kaye-Shuttleworth Papers on Education, 3. National Council for Educational Standards, Kenton, Middlesex.

Horton, R., and Finnegan, R., eds. 1973. *Modes of Thought*. London: Faber.

Hoyles, M., ed. 1977. *The Politics of Literacy*. London: Readers and Writers Publishing Co-operative.

Inhelder, B., and Piaget, J. 1958. *The Growth of Logical Thinking: From Childhood to Adolescence*. New York: Basic Books.

Jackson, L. A. 1974. The Myth of Elaborated and Restricted Codes. *Higher Education Review* 6, no. 2.

Jensen, A. 1969. Intelligence, Learning Ability and Socioeconomic Status. In S. Wiseman, eds., 1973.

―――― 1973. *Educability and Group Differences*. Edinburgh: Constable.

Kamin, L. 1974. *The Science and Politics of I.Q.* London: Wiley.

Keddie, N., ed. 1973. *Tinker, Tailor . . . The Myth of Cultural Deprivation*. London: Penguin.

Kelley, T. L. 1928. The Boundaries of Mental Life. In S. Wiseman, ed., 1973, excerpts from *Crossroads in the Mind of Man*, 63–82. Stanford: Stanford University Press.

The Kingman Report 1988. *Report of the Committee of Inquiry into the Teaching of English.* London: H.M.S.O.

Kleinig, T. 1982. *Philosophical Issues in Education.* London and Canberra: Croom Helm.

Labov, W. 1969. The Logic of Non-Standard English. In P.-P. Giglioli 1972, 179–215.

———— 1972. Some Principles of Linguistic Methodology. *Language in Society* 1, no. 1: 97–120.

Lakatos, I. 1970. Falsification and the Methodology of Scientific Research Programmes. In I. Lakatos, and A. Musgrave, eds., 1970.

Lakatos, I., and Musgrave, A., eds. 1970. *Criticism and the Growth of Knowledge.* Cambridge: Cambridge University Press.

Lee, V. 1981. *Social Aspects of Language,* pt. 2. Milton Keynes: The Open University Press.

Lévi-Strauss, C. 1962. *La Pensée Sauvage.* Paris: Editions Plon. Translated as *The Savage Mind.* London: Weidenfeld and Nicholson, 1966.

Lévy-Bruhl, L. 1910. *Les Fonctions Mentales dans les Sociétés Inférieures.* Paris: Alcan.

Lemmon, E. J. 1965. *Beginning Logic.* London, Edinburgh: Nelson.

Lenin, V. I. 1917. *The State and Revolution.* Moscow: Progress Publishers.

Locke, J. 1706. *An Essay Concerning Human Understanding,* vol. 2, bk. 2. Edited by J. Yolton. London: Dent, 1961.

Lyons, J. 1968. *An Introduction to Theoretical Linguistics.* Cambridge: Cambridge University Press.

Marx, K. 1858. *Pre-Capitalist Economic Formations.* Edited with an introduction by E. Hobsbawn. London: Lawrence and Wishart, 1964.

———— 1887. *Capital,* vol. 1. London: Lawrence and Wishart, 1964.

Marx, K., and Engels, F. 1846. *The German Ideology,* pt 1. Edited with an introduction by C. J. Arthur. London: Lawrence and Wishart, 1970.

MacMillan, C. A. 1982. *Women, Reason and Nature.* Oxford: Blackwell.

McPeck, J. 1981. *Critical Thinking and Education.* Oxford: Robertson.

Menyuk, P. 1988. *Language Development: Knowledge and Use.* Glenview, Ill., Boston, London: Scott Foresman.

Midgley, M. 1980. *Beast and Man.* London: Methuen.

The Norwood Report 1943. *Curriculum and Examinations in Secondary Schools.* London: H.M.S.O.

Nunally, J. 1981. *Psychometric Theory.* New Delhi: Tata McGraw Hill.

O'Hear, A. 1985. Review of "Beyond the Present and the Particular: A Theory of Liberal Education" by Charles Bailey. *Journal of Philosophy of Education* 19, no. 1: 146–51.

Olson, D. 1977. From Utterance to Text: The Bias of Language in Speech and Writing. *Harvard Educational Review* 47: 257–81.

Parkes, M., et al. 1989. *Design and Technology for Ages 5 to 16.* London: H.M.S.O.

Plato 1950. *The Republic.* Translated by J. Llewelyn Davies and D. J. Vaughan. London: MacMillan.

The Plowden Report 1967. *Children and their Primary Schools.* London, H.M.S.O.

Popper, Sir K. 1972. *Conjectures and Refutations.* London: Routledge.

Postman, N. 1970. *The Politics of Reading*. In N. Keddie, ed., 1973.

Potts, T. C. 1971. *Fregean Grammar*. Unpublished manuscript.

Raven, J. C. 1938. *Standard Progressive Matrices*. London: H. K. Lewis and Co. Ltd.

———— 1965. *Guide to Using the Mill Hill Vocabulary Scale with the Standard Progressive Matrices*. London: H. K. Lewis and Co. Ltd.

Robinson, W., and Rackstraw, S. 1972. *A Question of Answers*. London: Routledge.

Rosen, H. 1974. *Language and Class*. London: Falling Wall Press.

Rousseau, J. J. 1754. *A Dissertation on the Origin on Inequality among Men*. Translated with an introduction by G.D.H. Cole. London: Dent, 1968.

Rubinstein, D. 1981. *Wittgenstein and Marx*. London, Boston: Henley, Routledge.

Ryle, G. 1974. Intelligence and the Logic of the Nature–Nurture Issue: Reply to J. P. White. Proceedings of the Philosophy of Education Society of Great Britain 8, n. 1: pp. 52–60.

Salmon, W. 1963. *Logic*. Englewood Cliffs, N.J.: Prentice Hall.

Sapir, E. 1921. *Language: An Introduction to the Study of Speech*. London: Harvester, 1970.

Scribner, S., and Cole, M. 1978. Literacy without Schooling: Testing for Intellectual Effects. Vai Literacy Project, Working Paper 2, Rockefeller University, Laboratory of Comparative Human Cognition.

Simon, B. 1976. *Intelligence, Psychology, Education: A Marxist Critique*. London: Lawrence and Wishart.

Spearman, C. 1904. "General Intelligence" Objectively Determined and Measured. *American Journal of Psychology* 115: 201–92. Excerpts available in Wiseman, ed., 1973, 37–62.

———— 1927. *The Abilities of Man*. London: MacMillan.

Stubbs, M. 1976. *Language, Schools and Classrooms*. London: Methuen.

———— 1980. *Language and Literacy; The Sociolinguistics of Reading and Writing*. London: Routledge.

Tizard, B., and Hughes, M. 1984. *Young Children Learning*. London: Fontana.

Toft, B., and Kitwood, T. 1980. An Exploratory Study of Adolescent Speech Using Measures Derived from Bernstein's Theories. *Research in Education* 18: 9–34.

Tough, J. 1977a. *The Development of Meaning*. London: Allen and Unwin.

———— 1977b. *Talking and Learning*. London: Allen and Unwin.

Trudgill, P. 1975. *Accent, Dialect and the School*. London: Arnold.

Vernon, P. E. 1950. *The Structure of Human Abilities*. London: Methuen, 1950. Available as excerpts from chaps. 2 and 3 in S. Wiseman, ed., 1973, 101–14.

Vroon, P. A. 1980. *Intelligence: On Myths and Measurement*. Dordrecht: North Holland Publishing Company.

Waterland, L. 1988. *Read with Me*. 2d ed. Stroud: Thimble Press.

Wells, C. G. 1975. The Context of Children's Early Language Experience. *Educational Review* 27: 114–25.

———— 1977. Language Use and Educational Success: An Empirical Response to Joan Tough's "The Development of Meaning." *Research in Education* 18: 9–34.

———— 1981. Some Antecedents of Early Educational Attainment. *British Journal of Sociology of Education* 2, no. 2: 181–200.

———— 1987. *The Meaning Makers*. London: Hodder and Stoughton.

White, J. P. 1974. Intelligence and the Logic of the Nature–Nurture Issue. Proceedings of the Philosophy of Education Society of Great Britain 8, no. 1:1 30–51.

Whorf, B. L. 1956. *Language, Thought and Reality*. Cambridge, Mass., New York, London: M.I.T. Press.

Winch, C. A. 1983. Education, Literacy and the Development of Rationality. *Journal of Philosophy of Education* 17, no. 2: 187–200.

———— 1985a. Cooper, Labov, Larry and Charles. *Oxford Review of Education* 11, no. 2: 193–200.

———— 1985b. Verbal Deficit and Educational Success. *Journal of Applied Philosophy* 2, no. 1: 109–20.

———— 1987. The Curriculum and the Study of Reason. *Westminster Studies in Education* 10, 63–76.

———— 1988a. Ability, Intelligence and Practical Education. *Journal of Philosophy of Education* 22, no. 1: 35–44.

———— 1988b. The Honey Trap: The Social and Cognitive Adequacy of Language in Educational Contexts. *Journal of Applied Philosophy* 5, no. 2: 211–24.

Wiseman, S., ed. 1973. *Intelligence and Ability*. London: Penguin.

Wolfson, N. 1976. Speech Events and Natural Speech: Some Implications for Sociolinguistic Methodology. *Language in Society* 5, no. 2: 189–209.

Woods, R., and Barrow, R. 1975. *An Introduction to Philosophy of Education*. New York, London: Methuen.

Wootton, A. 1974. Talk in the Homes of Young Children. *Sociology* 8: 277–95.

Index